Omni-personal Luxury

"As one of the leaders in hard luxury retail, Bucherer has been working on its digital transformation and new ways of engaging with the customers which has been further accelerated with the COVID-19 situation. Omni-personal luxury is perfectly timed, providing essential insights on how to unlock the untapped value of exclusive personalized experience at scale as part of omni-channel scenarios. If you are involved in luxury business, this book is a must read!"

—Guido Zumbühl, CEO of *Bucherer*

"Covid has accelerated the preexisting structural shifts that were emerging, therefore this would be a first post-COVID view to give an outlook on how to manage the ongoing disruption in luxury. Personalisation has become a buzzword and the book acts as thought-leadership, addressing a broad audience of universities, associations, and professionals."

—François Delage, Former CEO of *DeBeers Jewellery, Paris, France*

Rebecca Schmitt • Arnaud Rossi
Albert Bensoussan

Omni-personal Luxury

How to Transform your Luxury Business for the Digital Age

Rebecca Schmitt
Munich, Germany

Arnaud Rossi
Geneva, Switzerland

Albert Bensoussan
Paris, France

ISBN 978-3-030-85768-4   ISBN 978-3-030-85769-1 (eBook)
https://doi.org/10.1007/978-3-030-85769-1

© The Editor(s) (if applicable) and The Author(s), under exclusive licence to Springer Nature Switzerland AG 2022
This work is subject to copyright. All rights are solely and exclusively licensed by the Publisher, whether the whole or part of the material is concerned, specifically the rights of translation, reprinting, reuse of illustrations, recitation, broadcasting, reproduction on microfilms or in any other physical way, and transmission or information storage and retrieval, electronic adaptation, computer software, or by similar or dissimilar methodology now known or hereafter developed.
The use of general descriptive names, registered names, trademarks, service marks, etc. in this publication does not imply, even in the absence of a specific statement, that such names are exempt from the relevant protective laws and regulations and therefore free for general use.
The publisher, the authors and the editors are safe to assume that the advice and information in this book are believed to be true and accurate at the date of publication. Neither the publisher nor the authors or the editors give a warranty, expressed or implied, with respect to the material contained herein or for any errors or omissions that may have been made. The publisher remains neutral with regard to jurisdictional claims in published maps and institutional affiliations.

This Palgrave Macmillan imprint is published by the registered company Springer Nature Switzerland AG.
The registered company address is: Gewerbestrasse 11, 6330 Cham, Switzerland

Preface

Dear Reader,

Written by passionate authors for an industry of passion, this book is an educated reflection based on our experiences in top management roles and consulting the leading companies in the luxury industry, combining our shared views on the upcoming challenges and opportunities.

Broadening Your Views

'Omni-personal luxury' is purposely not an academic or a scientific exercise. We diligently scouted the market for the latest global challenges and trends. More precisely, we gathered knowledge as part of our respective professional life and openly exchanged it with a number of c-level executives, IT and digital experts, as well as with a number of technology companies, to compile a broad view of the luxury industry's market trends. We think success is based on collaboration and knowledge, which is why we decided to share our insights, examples and references to open the eyes of the curious while centralising useful information for the knowledgeable.

The Ripples of Change

In the past 20 years, the world has contemplated the impact of digitalisation that is happening at various speeds in all industries and accelerated by new players attacking the market globally and/or locally. The rise of these new business models through 'online' whether it is about ordering, delivering or crowdsourcing/funding, or about converting 'buy' into 'rent', 'lease' or 'subscription', has been disruptive for the historical players. The codes behind what makes a business successful or the way companies should address their customers have been changing like never. The lines between traditional and technological companies are blurring (aren't all companies digital nowadays?), and the result is that yesterday's leaders and pillars of our economies are not today's and for sure will not be tomorrow's. Why would it be different for the luxury industry?

2020, the Year We Fast-Forwarded into a New Reality

Alongside the massive digital transformation happening across industries and markets, the luxury vessel has been keeping its course, leveraging century-old emotional and know-how codes entrenched in the success of the generated business. In the past ten years, we have experienced a number of online initiatives, but selling 'online', whether it was B2B or B2C, was not the prime strategy, and most companies invested in expanding the reach of professional fairs for their B2B business or in developing their proprietary retail network and footprint for those convinced that owning the relationship with the customer was the best way to generate growth—and it worked!

Although the luxury leaders had started their digital transformation, COVID-19 has created a 'digital necessity' and has 'put the church back in the centre of the village', as we say in French. Online presence and online customer engagement were the lifesavers in keeping the relationship with customers and compensating sales (with online sales) while stores were closed or while people could not travel. If you take a step back, this is just an acceleration of an unavoidable evolution given the changes we have seen in other industries, the expectations of the Asian customers (strategic area for growth) and, finally, the expectations of the new generations.

This 'new reality' growth and success will be based on a variety of ingredients, including relevant personal engagement across channels (online and offline), continuous customer lifecycle management, interacting with the new generations where they spend their time (i.e., gaming, virtual reality, social networks) and building cross-channel or industry experiences while committing and acting on sustainability. The biggest opportunity will be to orchestrate these channels and build the most relevant experiences for each individual customer. This is what we call 'Omni-personal luxury'.

We hope you enjoy this ride with us.

Geneva, Switzerland   Arnaud Rossi

Acknowledgement

We would like to acknowledge those persons who gave us the energy and constructive feedback to make this book happen.

First, we would like to thank the brilliant team at Palgrave Macmillan—in particular, Liz Barlow and Srishti Gupta.

Moreover, we would like to thank all our interview partners, namely Cyrille Vigneron, François-Henry Bennahmias, Georges Kern, Antonio Carriero and Kristian Tear. We thank Olivier Emery and François Delage for their valuable review.

We owe a big thanks to all the luxury brands and companies which kindly provided permission for us to print their images and screenshots, namely De Beers, Breitling, Oris, Forevermark, Courbet, Maison 203 and Henri Foucaud from Hapticmedia.

Our thanks also to our colleagues:

- Koen Deryckere, Christina Raab, Paddy Ananthanarayanan, Marco Huwiler, Lea Klipfel, Arnaud Dolignon, Tobias Nagel, Nico Michler and Bastian Rossberg, who supported us through the writing and the administrative process, allowing us to make this book a reality.
- Laurent Thoumine, Maria Mazzone and Andrea Ruzzi for their support and sharing their vision.
- Francesco De Maria, Domenico Vecchione, Petra Seipp, Steffen Bärenfänger and Dr Felix Wummer for their input in their respective areas of expertise.

On top, we highly appreciate the beta-reading of Pierre Sabot, Max Waddell, Francesca Italiano.

Finally, we thank our families for their love, tolerance and advice.

Markus Böttcher, Irmgard, Peter and Claude Schmitt—you were essential to make that dream real.

Thank you Mickaelle, Naomi and Gabriel Bensoussan as well as the extended Bensoussan family for your love, support and patience.

Thank you Plume, Eva and Mila for your love and support and who you are... 1+1=4 ;o)

You all contributed to making *Omni-personal Luxury* possible.

About This Book

Dear brand manager, IT and digital officer, innovation and experience expert, agency and curious reader, we welcome you! This book is made for you.

The omni-personal extends beyond the omni-channel. While the omni-channel is about the consistent and seamless experience across channels, the omni-personal is about relevant and individual experiences. It is about at-scale relationship building between a brand and its customers. 'Omni-personal luxury' targets an audience that is interested in the future of luxury. It provides deep insights for industry experts and those who would like to gain a better understanding of the required steps towards an omni-personal customer relationship, which is enabled by customer centricity, innovation, new business models and customer experience design.

Following a clear structure, seven chapters will answer your essential questions about who, why, how, what and when the omni-personal matters most in luxury. You will find the fundamental key aspects at the beginning of each chapter, including the leading practices and deep dives. We have written this book with luxury and premium brands in mind. For illustration, we will focus mostly but not only on use cases and examples from the jewellery and watch segment, which is also referred to as hard luxury.

At the beginning of this book, in **Chap.** 1, we investigate the macro trends and market dynamics. This will give us an understanding of how changing customer expectations are accelerating the omni-personal transformation towards the future of luxury.

Chapter 2 describes how luxury has followed its own rules throughout its history. Luxury has a special role to play in culture and society. Luxury today has many faces: from kings' heirs and status-driven logo collectors to magnificent bling-bling and even minimalist and timeless understatement. Luxury is a dynamic concept, but you can manage it, even in a world of continuous innovation and progress. Recently, we have started to devalue hardware and adore software in the same way that we devalue the material and adore experiences. This includes not only in-store but also online experiences: experiences everywhere, actually.

Chapter 3 explains that many luxury brands have approached the digital world carefully to protect cultural heritage and brand equity. Brand websites, shopping clubs and second-hand platforms have become a starting point to overcome an ambivalent relationship with the Internet. Meanwhile, social media platforms make omni-personal relationship building obligatory, giving customers their own voice.

In **Chap.** 4, we think customer-centrically and bring the omni-personal to prospective customer segments. On the one hand, this implies identifying the needs of millennials and the geographical contexts of the Asian growth markets, specifically China. On the other hand, these needs cause the rise of new consumption behaviours.

In **Chap.** 5, we derive a new omni-personal model to examine the transformation during the customer's journey. Here, you will also find omni-personal use cases and insights gained through experience and interviews with industry leaders.

In **Chap.** 6, we describe how to embed the omni-personal strategy into the business unit strategy, along with its technical, structural and organisational implications. We outline three approaches to kick off the omni-personal transformation: vertical integration, modular marketplaces and e-retail platforms and the full-stack ecosystem. To complete the picture, a matrix provides an overview of the brand reach and control linked to each approach.

Finally, do not jump to conclusions without asking about the next steps! In **Chap.** 7, we highlight that the omni-personal transformation starts with the assessment of an organisation's omni-personal maturity through the different channels and touchpoints within the customer journey. This involves five steps from the definition of the as-is and the target customer journey to the creation of an omni-personal transformation roadmap. Digital maturity has become a critical factor for luxury brands and conglomerates. This is the case today, and it will be especially important in the omni-personal world of tomorrow.

Luxury in general and jewellery and watches in particular are currently facing a period of disruption: quartz watches yesterday, smartwatches today and sustainable precious metals and stones tomorrow. Today, mobile phones show time and status to the world. Consequently, customers' wishes have rapidly evolved into needs, which reach far beyond the physical product. Will luxury as we know it today still be the luxury of tomorrow? How can we attract future target groups? Do we need a step change to prevent the luxury market from experiencing a Kodak moment? We are in fact conquering not the mountain but ourselves. In that sense, we are pleased to take you on this exciting journey towards the future of luxury. Be inspired, and be challenged! Enjoy reading, and start acting!

Contents

1	Introduction: The Future of Luxury	1
2	The Industry Is Special	17
3	Cautious Steps Towards Digital	35
4	Customer Centricity Is Key	51
5	Digital Transformation of the Omni-personal Customer Journey	63
6	How to Go Omni-personal	141
7	Conclusion: Embark on Your Journey to the Omni-personal Now	161
Bibliography		163
Index		171

About the Authors

Rebecca Schmitt is a Digital Transformation Manager at a global consulting firm and advises various luxury companies with a focus on customer experience, e-commerce, CRM and digital transformation. She lives in Munich, Germany. After her studies in Germany and France with a focus on the premium and luxury segment, she started her career at Amazon and worked as an independent digital consultant before she moved back into the corporate world. Over the last years she supported different luxury clients in Europe and Asia.

Arnaud Rossi brings more than 20 years of international consulting experience in large and complex transformation programmes such as Global Omni-channel/e-commerce/CRM implementation, Global ERP implementation, Operating Model transformation and Shared Service Organisation implementation. He has been working with global companies in consumer goods, retail and luxury sector since 2002 and is now leading the Consumer Goods and Luxury practice in Switzerland, Germany, Austria and Russia for a global consultancy firm.

About the Authors

Albert Bensoussan has worked for all leading luxury conglomerates (Richemont, LVMH, Kering) in his long executive career. Today he is the Vice Chairman of Bang & Olufsen and an independent advisor to luxury brands and financial investors, targeting the luxury sector.In his last position, he was CEO for the Luxury—Watches & Jewelry Division at the Kering Group. Before that, he had various executive roles at LVMH and Richemont, such as being the responsible global Director for Louis Vuitton's Watch and Jewelry business unit, the Sales and Marketing Director for the entire LVMH Watch & Jewelry Division, the President at Givenchy Couture in Japan, the Director of Leather Goods, Fashion Accessories and Eyewear Division at Givenchy Couture in France, and acting as the Director for Watches & Jewelry at Cartier.

Abbreviations

AR	Augmented Reality
ASMR	Autonomous Sensory Meridian Response
B2B	Business-to-Business
B2C	Business-to-Customer
C2C	Customer-to-Customer
CDJ	Customer Decision Journey Model
CDP	Customer Data Platform
CGI	Computer-Generated Images
CIO	Chief Information Officer
CNC	Computerised Numerical Control
CPQ	Configure, Price, Quote
CRM	Customer Relationship Management
CRO	Chief Relationship Officer
CSS	Cascading Style Sheet
D2C	Direct-to-Customer
DAM	Digital Asset Management
DMLS	Direct Metal Laser Sintering
DMP	Data Management Platform
ERP	Enterprise Resource Planning
FDM	Fused Deposition Modelling
FHH	Fondation de la Haute Horlogerie
Fondazione Altagamma	The Italian Luxury Goods Manufacturers' Industry Foundation
GDPR	General Data Privacy Regulation
Gen Y	Generation Y
Gen Z	Generation Z
GIA	Gemological Institute of America
GPS	Global Positioning System

HENRY	High Earners Not Rich Yet
HTML	Hyper-Text Markup Language
KOL	Key Opinion Leader
KPI	Key Performance Indicator
LOHAS	Lifestyle of Health and Sustainability
M&A	Mergers and Acquisitions
MDM	Master Data Management
MR	Mixed Reality
MVP	Minimal Valuable Product
NFC	Near-Field Communication
NIR	Near Infrared
NLP	Natural Language Processing
NPS	Net Promoter Score
OMS	Order Management System
PaaS	Platform as a Service
PIM	Product Information Management
POS	Point of Sale
QR	Quick Response
RFID	Radio-Frequency Identification
ROI	Return on Investment
SaaS	Software as a Service
SLA	Stereolithography
STISS	Swiss Technology inside Smart Sapphire
UTM	Urchin Tracking Module
VIP	Very Important Person
VR	Virtual Reality
YNAP	Yoox Net-a-Porter

List of Figures

Fig. 1.1	For many people the mobile has become the first screen (Image: Ipopba—stock.adobe.com)	5
Fig. 1.2	Touchpoints need to become digital to intensify the customer experience	11
Fig. 1.3	Omni-channel data as foundation of customer experience	13
Fig. 2.1	Maslow's pyramid of needs (Adapted from Maslow, 1943)	28
Fig. 3.1	Luxury and e-commerce—evolution in three phases, excluding Chinese platforms (see Sect. 3.2.2)	36
Fig. 3.2	The digital platform landscape in China	45
Fig. 5.1	The AIDA funnel model (Lewis, 1898)	65
Fig. 5.2	The CDJ customer decision journey model (McKinsey, 2009)	65
Fig. 5.3	The Omni-personal customer journey model	66
Fig. 5.4	Computer-generated image, Oris SA, Watch Inside a Watch, 2019 (Printed with Oris SA permission)	72
Fig. 5.5	Pop-up events intrigue with innovation and engaging experiences (Image: Fxquadro—stock.adobe.com)	77
Fig. 5.6	Games and gamified experiences are enjoying growing popularity, particularly among younger generations (Image: Gorodenkoff—stock.adobe.com)	81
Fig. 5.7	Virtual showcase platform, Accenture, 2021 (Printed with Accenture's permission)	86
Fig. 5.8	Visual search tool, Forevermark, 2021 (Printed with Forevermark's permission)	90
Fig. 5.9	Appointment-booking tool, Courbet, 2021 (Printed with Courbet's permission)	92

List of Figures

Fig. 5.10	Virtual try-on applications show huge potential to make the digital sales ceremony more interactive (Image: Andrey Popov—stock.adobe.com)	93
Fig. 5.11	Overview of sales scenarios	99
Fig. 5.12	Online product finder, Courbet, 2021 (Printed with Courbet's and Hapticmedia's permission)	102
Fig. 5.13	3D-printed jewellery, Maison 203, 2021 (Printed with Maison 203's permission)	104
Fig. 5.14	Seamless omni-channel experiences along channels and touchpoints	108
Fig. 5.15	End-to-end traceability	112
Fig. 5.16	Ten/ten collection, De Beers Group, 2021 (Printed with De Beers Group permission)	117
Fig. 5.17	The Net Promoter Score captures the recommendation likelihood of customers on a scale from 1 to 10 (Image: Olivier Le Moal - stock.adobe.com)	123
Fig. 5.18	Digital watch passport, Breitling, 2021 (Printed with Breitling's permission)	126
Fig. 5.19	Iterative process to deepen one-to-one relationships	128
Fig. 5.20	Illustrative set of common on-site and in-store KPIs along the customer journey	129
Fig. 5.21	Unlocking the potential of in-store customer monitoring	131
Fig. 6.1	The key elements of a business unit strategy	142
Fig. 6.2	The omni-personal strategy	143
Fig. 6.3	The omni-personal and business unit strategies affect each other	144
Fig. 6.4	The intended brand reach and control define the approach	157

1

Introduction: The Future of Luxury

Key Aspects

- The personal relationship is at the centre of the luxury strategy.
- Business transformation is addressing new customer needs.
- Customers expect whatever goods and services they want wherever and whenever they want them.
- The COVID-19 crisis provides a glimpse into the crystal ball to predict the future.
- Luxury needs to exploit the potential of new retail in a brand-consistent and customer-relevant way.
- Future market growth in luxury is predicted to be driven by China and e-commerce.

The personal luxury market (i.e., watches, jewellery, leather goods, clothing, fragrance and skincare) increased from €77 billion in 1995 to €281 billion in 2019.[1] However, following the outbreak of COVID-19, the market shrank by 20 to 35 per cent in 2020 but is predicted to bounce back to €330 to €370 billion by 2025.[2] This estimate already takes the correction due to the COVID-19 crisis into account. Traditionally, the growth potential in luxury has mainly been a result of geographic expansion and brand or line extension. In contrast, the predicted growth until 2025 will be mainly driven by the Chinese market, the growing relevance of the online distribution channel and the readiness of brands to transform themselves in favour of their customers.

Think about yourself. How many items do you own? Today, the average European citizen has around 10,000 items. By comparison, only 100 years ago, the average amount of owned goods was 180 items per person.[3] About 100 years ago, travel was a special adventure that could take days or weeks, depending on the destination. Commercial flights have been available since 1914, but economy class did not exist until 1950. Previously, flying was pure luxury.[4] In 2019, 38.9 million flights were recorded. The 40.3 million flights forecast to take place in 2020 were cut to 23.1 million due to the COVID-19 crisis.[5]

Moreover, the number of billionaires is growing globally. In particular, the United States and China are leading the list of the richest people. The Hurun Report 2020 concluded that the COVID-19 outbreak caused a mini-boom in pharmaceuticals and online entertainment, which helped China to create three times more billionaires than the United States in 2019.[6]

These figures indicate that our lifestyle has changed significantly and so have our expectations. We have arrived at a point at which we have to ask ourselves some questions. Just how much ownership is necessary? How much travelling is required? In addition, how much is healthy for our ego and environment? We challenge and are challenged on green thinking and exploiting the healing elixir of a circular economy. We are starting to measure our consumption behaviour in terms of sustainability for the future of the planet, and our children are becoming active advocates of our maturity. Overconsumption is moving into a dim light, especially consumption that appears to be elitist and superfluous. Is luxury at risk? Is luxury still appropriate? Some might ask whether there is still a place for luxury in a world on the brink of eco-exodus. Is luxury following zeitgeist?

In this world, transformation is a matter of survival. There are always industries that move faster than others, disrupting business models and creating added value for customers. The luxury industry is not disruptive, but no industry knows better how to engage and evoke emotions. Luxury has existed for many centuries and always found a way to meet the needs of its time. Today, there is a risk that some brands may be lagging behind, while, for others, this is the perfect time to make a difference.

1.1 Why the Omni-personal Approach Is the Key for Luxury

When Alfred Cartier handed the business over to his sons, Louis, Pierre and Jacques, he attached the condition that each of the three existing Cartier branch offices should be managed by one of the sons.[7] Mr Cartier was perfectly aware that personal relationships were a key element of selling luxury goods to the royals and wealthy elites of his time. Selling luxury goods requires you to know as much as possible about your customers. Who is making the final decision? Is it a gift? Is she in favour of diamonds or pearls? What are the purpose and event of the visit? Is she his companion or his mistress? Those were key data for addressing the customer appropriately and discreetly.

In another example, Burberry has introduced data analytics initiatives, such as 'Customer 360',[8] which invites customers to share their shopping histories and preferences with the brand. Upon entering a Burberry store in China, customers might be surprised to find that the sales associate already knows their colour and product preferences. Some appreciate the ability to become immediately involved in a conversation about red boots matching the last purchase of a red belt, which is part of the same collection. For others, this experience might appear to be bordering on scary or invasive.

Customer data are a big responsibility, but when used correctly, they are a powerful tool. The world of Alfred Cartier was entirely different from our world, but the need for personalisation remains unchanged. The challenge is transforming today's big data into smart data to offer personalisation at scale. Just like customers in 1900, modern customers expect to be welcomed into a shop in the same individual way. As a future customer, you will expect to be recognised, welcomed, served, understood and remembered across channels and touchpoints in a consistent way. This is what we call the omni-personal approach to secure the human touch and connect in our interactions.

1.1.1 Customer Expectations Are Changing Once Again

Several macro trends are influencing the way in which customers expect the perfect shopping experience:

- Seamless omni-channel
- Mobile first
- Experience
- (Omni-) personalisation
- Sustainability

Seamless Omni-channel

You are a customer. You live the omni-channel way: you try on your favourite products via the mobile app, order online, pick up the order in store, return the product to another store and expect to receive personalised advertising, which takes care to understand that you are no longer interested in the product that you returned the other day. It follows natural logic that customers expect companies to follow omni-channel principles. Nowadays, 70 per cent of luxury purchases are influenced by online interaction.[9] People gain inspiration on social media platforms, open the brand's newsletter on their phone and search the Web for certain articles of interest before they decide to purchase online or in store.

The in-store experience remains central to the luxury industry, but customers expect brand accessibility of whatever they are interested in, wherever and whenever they want it. This is a consequence of socio-cultural change, globalisation and technological progress. The objective of the omni-channel is clearly to provide a seamless and consistent journey across online and offline channels and touchpoints. This also calls for the integration of in-store, digital, social, mobile and even integrated third-party networks.

The need for a seamless omni-channel approach is emphasised by modern customer behaviour: interacting simultaneously across different devices, for instance browsing through product descriptions on the iPad while watching television and discussing the choice with a best friend on the phone, is a common practice today. In particular, younger generations are trained to multi-task across devices.

Mobile First
Since 2016, we have observed an orientation towards applications and smartphone commerce.[10] For many people, and even many countries, the mobile has become the first screen and increasingly the preferred method of payment, using services such as PayPal, Amazon Payment, Alipay and WeChat Pay, which are both fast and convenient (Fig. 1.1).

In the luxury segment, 98 per cent of customers have their own smartphone. Surprisingly, this figure is consistent across the age range, from millennials to baby boomers. While millennials own on average 4 mobile devices and use them for 17.5 hours per week, baby boomers own 3.5 mobile devices on average and use them for 16.4 hours per week.[11] That is not a dramatic gap and highlights that this is a real macro trend.

Experience
While digital content strategies were previously the focus, designing differentiated digital experiences will be key in the future. Online channels will be affected by the move towards digital, while the physical in-store experience

Fig. 1.1 For many people the mobile has become the first screen (Image: Ipopba—stock.adobe.com)

will evolve through digital extension. Merging the two worlds into a seamless and consistent journey is known as 'phygital', which corresponds to the concept of the omni-channel.

Augmented, extended and virtual reality applications are increasingly blending into our day-to-day life, enriching our experience by supporting our imagination and simplifying our decisions. Examples include virtual try-on applications, avatars and virtual runways, which are designed to approach the target audience engagingly, often including elements of gamification.

(Omni-) Personalisation

Personalisation is a complex trend that has many dimensions throughout the whole value chain: from product personalisation, thanks to innovative configuration tools and 3D printing, to the capturing of customer data on purchase preferences to apply data intelligence and analytics to predict behaviour and recommend the most relevant products and to geo-localisation via GPS to send personalised push notifications to users' mobile phone when they are close to the store.

It is clear that these initiatives will make the product, service, communication and experience personal and therefore relevant to the target audience. While the omni-channel focuses on consistency and seamlessness across channels and touchpoints, the omni-personal has an additional layer to ensure relevance to the individual customer. That relevance is the basis of true customer engagement. And we should not forget to listen to the customer carefully. In a brand monologue, brands tend to understand what they like to hear. When brands cultivate an open dialogue, they learn to accept a 'No', without losing something. Indeed, it is a question of respect to gain the customer's trust.

Sustainability

Sustainability is indispensable and affects the whole value chain. On the one hand, it is a matter of transparency; on the other hand, it is a matter of consequences and actions derived from that knowledge. First, we can enable end-to-end traceability from raw material (including fair trade and labour conditions) to semi-finished and finished goods in warehouses, distribution channels, stores and finally customers' homes to support after-sales services. Second, we need to translate the knowledge gained about the resource origin, production processes and customer demand into a sustainable business model.

In luxury, there are many different points of view. Some identify the huge contrast between luxury (which is associated with immaterial quality, mystery, magic and dreams) and sustainability (which is associated with pure product quality, transparency, fairness and reality). Meanwhile, others say that, in true luxury, secrets are not needed because the high quality stands for itself and there is nothing to hide. Furthermore, luxury products are made to last for eternity, and what is more sustainable than a product that can be passed from one generation to the next? Without giving a final answer to that question, the social, political, economic and cultural discussion has certainly promoted the birth of new business models, such as rental and resale. The rise of those business models illustrates the increasing importance of sustainability and responsibility along the value chain.

The call for more sustainability and circularity triggered especially in the fashion industry a radical way of rethinking. Various start-ups are working on solutions how to use and reuse resources more responsible. One of those is 'Fashion-for-Good'. While the number of discarded textiles is continuously growing, the initiative targets to establish a platform to support an efficient recycling infrastructure. The highly manual sorting lacks often accuracy due to missing material composition and label information. Hence, Fashion-for-Good established a comprehensive textile waste analysis based on Near Infrared (NIR) technology, mapped with textile recycler's capabilities. That extended understanding of textile composition leads to an increase in reusable textiles and opens up new revenue streams for sorters through circular economy principles. On top, the textile waste can be reduced. However, that example tackles the challenge in the end of the value chain. Sustainability needs a holistic approach, and therefore, brands put also more and more attention on a responsible resource selection in the beginning of the product life cycle—even during the product design phase.

Continuous Innovation: Living with Ongoing Change
Understanding the changing customer demands and major trends is essential. Beyond that, designing suitable and differentiating experiences calls for continuous innovation. It implies the acceptance of impermanence in the sense that we are facing changes at all times. Cartier's CEO, Cyrille Vigneron, puts this in the following words:

> Despite this (change), we tend to see stability as the norm and change as the exception. Yet the world evolves faster than ever. To live in this world serenely, we need to embrace impermanence.[12]

Do you have a vision on the future world where you want to live? What would exceed your expectations? Do you understand your customers better than they understand themselves? This is our psychological and creative challenge.

In China, there is a visionary pilot project, Changsha IFS Mall.[13] The mall features a range of international luxury and fashion brands. So far, you are thinking 'another mall', but here is the cherry on the cake: the mall offers the mobile app iGO, the first mixed-reality (MR) shopping navigator, to customers in 5G, unlocking an intelligent and personalised customer experience with special offers, augmented reality and an embedded treasure hunt game. Users' location is recognised accurately and in real time, which allows perfectly timed communication and interactions via their mobile phone. Without downloading another application, customers can easily access, with one click, the official Changsha IFS WeChat page to start shopping. The innovation of the mall is that it brings the latest and greatest in phygital together into one immersive experience. This is an example of traditional retail moving into phygital. However, luxury brands are increasingly competing not only on experiences designed by other luxury brands and retailers but also against digital-first ecosystems,[14] such as those of Amazon and Alibaba.

1.1.2 Luxury Dives into New Retail

Alibaba calls it new retail, while JD refers to it as boundary-less retail. WeChat talks about smart retail, and Amazon refers to thinking backwards from the customer.[15] These concepts build on customer centricity across channels and touchpoints. These technology giants are building ecosystems to serve customer needs following a holistic approach. They have discovered needs that previously we were not even aware existed. Who would have thought that a company like Amazon would accompany you through all the phases of everyday life, from digital grocery shopping to evening video streaming to AWS cloud-hosted enterprise software? This is what is happening. Furthermore, born digital, these companies are now extending their footprint towards brick-and-mortar shops. Alibaba has launched Freshippo, the supermarket of the future, while Amazon has realised a comparable idea with Amazon Go.

Typical Amazon customers will not understand why they may have to wait for days or even weeks for a certain luxury good ordered online when they can receive articles ordered via Amazon within the same day or even the same hour. This is the reason why the luxury marketplace Farfetch has launched same-day delivery in selected metropoles.[16] We have now reached the point at which customers take it for granted that they can obtain what they want when and how they want it. The necessary and expected have changed. Younger generations are even accelerating that change because they are not attracted by old retail. They grew up with iPads in their hands and know more about virtual services than about animals in the forest. What baby boomers still call a desire has become a need for Gen Y and Gen Z.

Luxury brands are not new retail experts by default because their original core competence lies in the unique product design, creation and manufacturing excellence of outstanding creations. The distribution network maturity varies widely between brands. That depends on their history and those that rely on their corporate strategy. Some of them have no retail channel at all and do not see any need to change. Accordingly, one size does not fit all.

For those who were looking for synergies in centralised and regional support functions, joining a luxury conglomerate became a possible option. Synergies are one of the reasons for the many cases of market consolidation and merger and acquisition (M&A) activity over the last few decades. Besides logistics, warehousing, human resources and media buying, IT, ERP and digital tools benefit from the potential of scalability.[17] This point is important because scalability and human and financial resources are enablers of an efficient move towards new retail. Investment in an internal tool landscape is one of the possible strategies. Another strategy is targeted investment in big digital players, the setting up of joint ventures or the acquisition of marketplace platforms to accelerate and strengthen the positioning in the digital world. Some examples follow:

- *Targeted investment*: Chanel set up a strategic partnership with the global luxury e-commerce platform Farfetch. In 2021, Kering invested in the second-hand platform Vestiaire Collective.
- *Joint venture*: In 2018, Yoox Net-a-Porter (YNAP) launched the joint venture Feng Mao in collaboration with Alibaba. In 2020, Alibaba and Richemont announced that they would team up with Farfetch.
- *Acquisition of a marketplace platform*: Since 2018, Richemont has been the major shareholder of YNAP. In 2017, the private equity fund Apax acquired the fashion retailer MatchesFashion.

Regardless of the strategy chosen, luxury customers have new expectations in terms of brands, consumption and experience. Authenticity in addressing these needs must be credible. Meanwhile, credibility is necessary to be meaningful to the customer. Meaning is required to generate sales: that is just as true in new, smart, boundary-less retail as it was in old retail. For this reason, there is only one direction to go: forward!

1.1.3 COVID-19 Is Accelerating the Change

People will stop traveling, the feel-good factor will disappear. People will no longer go to the shopping center. We like to forget what happened at the beginning of the last century (…) And back then there were no airplanes that could have carried the virus around the world at lightning speed. I have to act as if it could happen at any time.
—Johann Rupert, Chairman of Richemont, Interview in 2005[18]

'The pandemic made us accelerate the work, and double down on resources and competences in the digital field', stated Kristian Tear, CEO of Bang & Olufsen, in our questionnaire. Black swan events, such as the financial crisis in 2008 and COVID-19, push economies and companies into extreme situations overnight. Personal luxury goods have experienced a double-digit revenue decrease. At the beginning of the crisis, people worldwide believed COVID-19 to be a Chinese problem, only affecting the supply chain; then, it became a global pandemic and a global demand issue. Around the globe, manufacturers and stores temporarily shut down, and the whole distribution network was affected. However, the closed doors of physical stores increased the pressure to open virtual doors. During a crisis, it is vital for brands to react in an agile way with digital priorities and a rich innovation mindset.[19] Antonio Carriero, Chief Digital and Technology Officer of Breitling, outlined in our interview:

After 25 years of Digital, COVID-19 triggered an additional sense of urgency about transforming the operating model of any company in the retail arena. At Breitling the Digital (Business) Transformation started already in 2017, encompassing all the dimensions of our value chain. (…) We proved during COVID-19 that we were on the right path.

Three major focus areas have been identified in several post-COVID-19 studies:

- Digital experience
- China first
- Market disruption

Digital Experience
Offline touchpoints are at risk of losing their momentum as face masks and suppressed breathlessness are shortening in-store visits and flattening the customer experience (Fig. 1.2). The customer experience can be reintensified by translating offline touchpoints into digital formats.

The virtual possibility appears in different layers, from virtual content production of computer-generated images to platforms for virtual live-streaming events and stores, including showrooms and runways. LVMH, Kering and other luxury companies have launched virtual showrooms,[20] and the Paris and Milan fashion weeks have moved online. For the Milan digital fashion week, Accenture and Microsoft collaborated to provide a digital platform to support Camera Nazionale della Moda.[21] Even auction houses have successfully started digital sales in customers' living rooms. Impressive examples were the winning online bid on a US$1.5 million Patek Philippe Ref. 2499 or Sotheby's auction of a royal tiara signed Musy for CHF1.5 million.[22] Musy was promoted via an Instagram activation in May 2021. Thanks to an Instagram augmented-reality filter, the tiara has been tried on virtually over 22,000 times. Especially in China, social commerce is experiencing high demand; platforms like Yizhibo, Xiaohongshu, Taobao and WeChat have proved their success in live-streaming events.

1 Introduction: The Future of Luxury

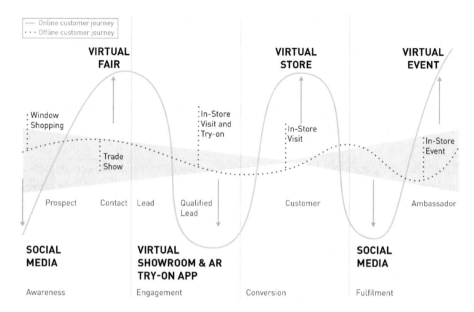

Fig. 1.2 Touchpoints need to become digital to intensify the customer experience

China First

Richemont and other luxury conglomerates keep reporting positive signs from China, thanks to reopened stores and so-called revenge shopping.[23] Customers have started to compensate themselves for the deprivation experienced during the lockdown period with luxury goods. This positive news indicates that the recovery phase in China is significantly shorter than in other regions of the world, even if the United States are recovering faster as initially predicted due to the progress in vaccination.

Moreover, the travel restrictions imply that brands provide local experiences in China, including second- and third-tier cities.[24] By 2025, the Chinese market is predicted to account for around half of the global luxury spending.[25]

Market Disruption

Based on the market shakeout, many companies and business models are being put to the test in terms of sustainability, efficiency, innovation spirit and agility. Companies with a low level of maturity in those key areas will struggle to survive the crisis, which implies that further consolidation will occur through M&As. On top, consumption behaviour is becoming more conscious as the disposable income is shrinking in many households. This also supports the rise of new business models focusing on sustainability and the circular economy.

1.2 The Industry Needs to Grasp the Potential of New Retail

Over the last pages, we have considered the macro trends, market dynamics and accelerators affecting the luxury industry. In this chapter, we focus on the vision and future of luxury. However, it is now time to elaborate on the full potential of new retail because, as a brand, you should be where the customers expect you to be: everywhere and at all times. At first, this sounds like an impossible mission. Furthermore, there are certain specifics in the luxury industry, including rarity and exclusivity, which mean that we need to be more precise.

While omni-channel luxury could be misunderstood in the sense that a brand needs to activate all channels to be present on all of them, it is fundamental to clarify that the most important point is to stay brand consistent across the active channels. To achieve this, a brand needs to gain a clear understanding of the relevant channels and touchpoints. In particular, in terms of social media, forums and product review platforms, it is necessary to look carefully to capture useful information on your customers.

As an extension to the omni-channel, the omni-personal means leveraging the relationship by entering a dialogue with the prospect or customer. Individual customer data are integrated to create a brand- and customer-consistent experience. In that way, customer data include information captured throughout customers' journey or derived from their sales history as follows: purchased products; product configurations made; products on wish lists; preferences for certain materials, colours, styles and values, such as sustainability; time duration between purchases; distribution preference; key customer dates, such as birthdays and wedding days; newsletter preferences; contact preferences; home addresses; nearby stores; and so on.

In conclusion, you should be where the customer expects you to be, which is everywhere, where to ensure a brand-consistent and customer-relevant dialogue (Fig. 1.3). To translate this into a metaphor, you need to avoid appearing like an emperor who has no clothes. In Asia, people talk about losing face in embarrassing moments. As a brand, you have a face as well as a name, and

1 Introduction: The Future of Luxury

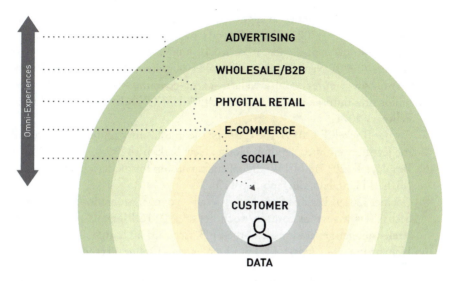

Fig. 1.3 Omni-channel data as foundation of customer experience

both matter for your business every day. Therefore, people sell to people. Dress up and show your face to follow the new retail approach in an omni-personal way!

As mentioned at the beginning of this chapter, luxury has certain specifics. In the next chapter, we will investigate what makes luxury so special.

Notes

1. Sherman L (2020) The next wave of luxury e-commerce. In: The business of fashion. https://www.businessoffashion.com/education/courses/case-study-luxury-ecommerce-online-retail, p 2. Accessed 30 April 2020.
2. Bain & Company (2020) Bain-Altagamma 2020 worldwide luxury market monitor. In: The Diamond Loupe. https://www.thediamondloupe.com/sites/awdcnewswall/files/attachments/Bain-Altagamma%20Luxury%20Study%2019th%20Edition.pdf. Accessed 18 November 2020.
3. Kern S (2014) Wie viel ist genug? https://www.rnz.de/panorama/magazin_artikel,-Magazin-Wie-viel-ist-genug-_arid,20959.html. Accessed 26 April 2020.
4. LoveExploring (2018) How air travel has changed in the last 100 years. https://www.loveexploring.com/gallerylist/71818/how-air-travel-has-changed-in-the-last-100-years. Accessed 28 February 2021.

5. Statista (2020) Number of flights performed by the global airline industry from 2004 to 2021. https://www.statista.com/statistics/564769/airline-industry-number-of-flights/. Accessed 10 June 2020.
6. Reuters (2020) New Chinese billionaires outpace U.S. by 3 to 1: Hurun. https://www.reuters.com/article/us-china-economy-wealth/new-chinese-billionaires-outpace-u-s-by-3-to-1-hurun-idUSKCN20K0YB. Accessed 26 February 2021.
7. Cartier Brickell F (2019) The Cartiers: the untold story of the family behind the jewellery empire. Random House, New York, p 147.
8. Beauloye F (2017) SHINE: digital craftsmanship for modern luxury brands. Michael Hanrahan, Singapore, p 113.
9. Gartner (2019) Lessons from luxury retail—younger generation lead the way. https://www.gartner.com/en/documents/3905168/lessons-from-luxury-retail-younger-generations-lead-the-, p 3. Accessed 20 March.
10. Heinemann G (eds) (2019) Der neue Online Handel. Springer, Wiesbaden, p 139.
11. McKinsey & Company (2018) The age of digital Darwinism. https://www.mckinsey.com/~/media/McKinsey/Industries/Retail/Our%20Insights/Luxury%20in%20the%20age%20of%20digital%20Darwinism/The-age-of-digital-Darwinism.pdf, p 5. Accessed 3 April 2021.
12. Vigneron C (2020) LinkedIn post, 4 February, cited with permission.
13. Changsha IFS (2020) Changsha IFS creates iGO, the first MR shopping navigator in China, to open smart shopping with one click. In: Cision PR Newswire. https://www.prnewswire.com/news-releases/changsha-ifs-entwickelt-igo-den-ersten-mr-einkaufsnavigator-in-china-der-intelligentes-einkaufen-mit-einem-klick-ermoglicht-819629444.html. Accessed 16 December 2020.
14. Santhiram S (2020) How luxury brands can leverage e-commerce to bounce back post-COVID-19. https://www.luxurysociety.com/en/articles/2020/04/how-can-luxury-brands-their-e-commerce-game-post-covid19/. Accessed 27 April 2020.
15. Dudarenok AG, Zakkour M (2019) New retail born in China going global: how Chinese tech giants are changing global commerce. Independently published, pp 48, 107.
16. Chevalier M, Gutsatz M (eds) (2019) Luxury retail and digital management. Wiley, New Jersey, Location 2070.
17. Kapferer, J (2015) Kapferer on luxury: how luxury brands can grow yet remain rare. Kogan Page, London, p 214.
18. Kowalsky M. (2005) Johann Rupert: «Ich bin der Fluglotse der Egos». https://www.handelszeitung.ch/geld/johann-rupert-ich-bin-der-fluglotse-der-egos. Accessed 12 April 2021.
19. Langer D (2020) How luxury brands can win during a crisis. https://jingdaily.com/how-luxury-brands-can-win-during-a-crisis. Accessed 22 April 2020.

20. Guiltbault L (2020) LVMH and Kering's new battlefield is online. https://www.voguebusiness.com/companies/lvmh-and-kerings-new-battlefield-is-online-covid-19. Accessed 12 June 2020.
21. Accenture (2020) Accenture and Microsoft collaborate to provide digital platform to support Camera Nazionale Della Moda Italiana's Milan digital fashion week. https://newsroom.accenture.com/news/accenture-and-microsoft-collaborate-to-provide-digital-platform-to-support-camera-nazionale-della-moda-italianas-milan-digital-fashion-week.htm. Accessed 14 July 2020.
22. Corzine M (2020) Philips Watches Head of Digital Strategy: 'Collectors were quick to accept digital sales'. https://www.luxurysociety.com/en/articles/2020/06/phillips-watches-head-digital-strategy-collectors-were-quick-accept-digital-sales/. Accessed 25 June 2020 and Vachaudez C (2021) Musy—Magnificent and Historic Natural pearl and diamond tiara. https://www.sothebys.com/en/buy/auction/2021/magnificent-jewels-and-noble-jewels-part-i/magnificent-and-historic-natural-pearl-and-diamond-2. Accessed 5 June 2021.
23. Richemont (2021) Richemont consolidated financial statements. https://www.richemont.com/en/home/investors/results-reports-presentations/, p 84. Accessed 5 June 2021.
24. Achille A, Zipser D (2020) A perspective for the luxury-goods industry during—and after—coronavirus. https://www.mckinsey.com/industries/retail/our-insights/a-perspective-for-the-luxury-goods-industry-during-and-after-coronavirus. Accessed 1 April 2020.
25. Bain & Company (2020) Bain-Altagamma 2020 worldwide luxury market monitor. In: The Diamond Loupe. https://www.thediamondloupe.com/sites/awdcnewswall/files/attachments/Bain-Altagamma%20Luxury%20Study%2019th%20Edition.pdf. Accessed 18 November 2020.

2

The Industry Is Special

Key Aspects

- Luxury is a socio-cultural code that is commonly understood.
- Luxury and its interpretation are constantly changing according to the context.
- The context for interpreting luxury is defined by time, culture and society.
- The interpretation of modern luxury is characterised by its democratisation, romantic consumerism, globalisation and digitalisation.
- High-end luxury is differentiated based on perceived scarcity, high-end quality and price, product aesthetics and uniqueness as well as symbolism.
- Customers desire luxury as it makes them feel good through positive emotions.
- Luxury consumption is intrinsically and extrinsically motivated.
- Luxury is an experience.
- The experience tends to be immaterial, and personal perception matters.
- Luxury shares common elements with art and religion.

Luxury means selling dreams, and like every dream, it depends on one's personal perception and interpretation, particularly of what is luminous or boundless. Both facets are part of the origin of the word 'luxury'—the Latin root word *lux* translates into 'light', while the Latin *luxuria* relates to self-indulgence and opulence. Finding one common definition of luxury is impossible, as it means something different to every person on the planet. The customers and the changing definition of luxury are thus identified as the biggest threats disrupting luxury.[1] Luxury is also close to another socio-cultural phenomenon—art. Through the consumption of luxury, users become connoisseurs and elevate their taste in a figurative sense. Luxury creations, often an outcome of artistic craftsmanship, radiate their glamour to their owners or consumers. Luxury is thus a socio-cultural code, transmitting messages between the sender and the receiver. The significant advantage of codes is that they are commonly understood across regions, languages and cultures, and this understanding is only possible because the sender and the receiver have a common toolbox for encoding and decoding messages. This toolbox consists of experience, emotion and education.

The value of gold is emblematic in connection to luxury: the metal is rare and too soft to be used in the production of functional tools. Nevertheless, it takes a lot of energy and effort to work the metal into ornaments, and only in the last step does the shiny finish appear when it is polished. Gold has been a status symbol for millennia. Besides being beautiful, its only purpose is to express superiority. That message is decoded in a particular cultural, social and emotional context in which gold is not affordable for everyone. It is difficult to find, and its colour and texture are unique. When the context changes,[2] the perception of luxury adjusts under that influence. That could threaten us if we invent an artificial way of mining gold and the precious material is no longer a rarity. This situation happened for pearls around 1930 based on the commercial rise of cultured pearls and is perhaps similar to the story of lab-grown diamonds.[3]

Luxury is a dynamic concept that changes constantly over time, depending on the societal and cultural contexts. Luxury is thus specific and demanding as the segment calls for its brands to be unique in terms of products, experience, communication and emotional value. To maintain the luxury code and update it constantly, we look to its history, outlining its main characteristics and its differentiators from fashion, premium and 'masstige' products. The latter term describes a downward brand extension that translates into prestige for the masses. We then analyse the emotional value and complete this chapter with a definition of luxury that will be at the centre of the further considerations in this book.

2.1 In History, Luxury Has Always Played a Special Role

There have always been the happy few who can afford to consume luxury items while others can only dream of them. As a logical consequence, luxury has been personalised for as long as it has existed. Even though luxury is not the source of social inequality, it highlights differences. Throughout history, the insignia of power has been reserved for social elites: royal houses, aristocrats, merchants, industrialists or executives. With the personalisation of luxury, this gap has been bridged. In addition to the dimension of extraordinarily exclusive, rare products or services and their role as social markers, two further dimensions of luxury have evolved: luxury as a market that is analysed annually by international consultancies and luxury as a business model and strategy to differentiate brands from each other.[4] The latter refers to aspects such as the full control of the value chain, distribution, experience and pricing as well as excellence in manufacturing, personalisation, communication and marketing. Luxury has doubtless always adapted to its time and society. Are you ready for a deep dive into its evolution and history?

2.1.1 Origins of Luxury: The Dose Makes the Poison

Luxury is a necessity that begins where necessity ends.
—Coco Chanel

Origins of Luxury: Raw Materials
As the example of gold showed, luxury is rooted in the beginnings of civilisation, when the rarity of materials defined luxury. Seashells, amber, ivory, jade and gold were traded and worn as jewellery. It is human nature to love the beautiful, and people have always enjoyed dressing up to impress, even when the tools were limited. As soon as people were used to luxury, it became a necessity. When humans settled down, they started to collect things and to link their emotions and memories to material goods. They also started to embellish raw materials through manual processing.

Ancient Societies: Design Matters
Design works magic. A raw diamond is just a milky stone, but with the perfect cut, the total value of the stone increases, even if the colour, clarity and size do not match the perfect conditions. In ancient societies, the design of products extended the value of raw materials. In ancient Egypt, pharaohs became accustomed to thinking in terms of pyramids to show off their power and status during their lifetime and beyond. The shape of a pyramid expressed eternity. The celebration of splendour during life and the ritualistic perfection for immortalising oneself in the afterlife are particularly noteworthy.[5] This indicates that religion and luxury were interconnected, as believing in gods or even in oneself gave deeper meaning to human life.

Millennia later, Diogenes (probably the first convinced minimalist) lived in a barrel and criticised the pompous and ostentatious life of the elites. Sparta, the Greek military power, did not need to be taught the simple way of life because those who wanted to win had to exercise iron discipline. Simplicity was often forced, but a real man maintained positivity despite having few possessions. Showing off material wealth was the privilege of royals and aristocrats. Criticism of this regime increased under the Romans, as Seneca and Cicero predicted the decline of the Roman Empire while Nero held riotous orgies. Only a new religion helped to return society to a just sense of proportion.

The Middle Ages: Worship of Craftsmanship
During the Middle Ages, luxury maintained its status as something superfluous. The church allowed glamour only within the house of God, while believers hoped for an easy afterlife in heaven. Nevertheless, craftsmanship and merchandising gained power. Within cities, merchants positioned themselves in the same neighbourhood as their competitors.[6] This simplified their customers' choices by enabling comparison. Comparison also called for differentiation, so craftsmen and early jewellers fell in love with complex ornaments, as it was generally known that the creation of such details required extra time. In China, the Ming dynasty imposed luxury laws to define the dress code for the nation's hierarchies: for example, head jewellery with gold and jade were not permitted for non-elites, although caps with crystal and scented woods were allowed.[7]

The Renaissance and the Modern Era: Signed by Artists
The art world changed with the painter Albrecht Dürer as he began to sign his paintings with his name. The name of the creator was thus immortalised as part of the artwork, and the artist's name became a symbol of value. Other industries followed this example, and family names became synonyms for special expertise. Only an artist knew exactly how to invest time and effort to transform a piece of gold into a piece of art. Today, we refer to those signs of authenticity when we talk about brands.

Modern Revolutions: Perfection at Scale
The French Revolution in 1789 became the epitome of the declared goal—freedom, equality, fraternity. It was a clear message to the elites and their provocative consumption of luxury. Democracies were founded, but luxury was not yet

democratic: only the target audience of luxury changed. This was obvious when, 100 years after the French Revolution, Alfonso XIII, the King of Spain, looked at a Cartier price tag for 1.25 million francs: 'Only the nouveaux riches can afford such luxuries … we kings are the nouveaux pauvres of today!'[8]

In parallel, the Industrial Revolution changed people's life and work dramatically. Production at scale was no longer a dream, and ambition moved towards the perfection of clean and functional product design. This evolution would find its peak in the early twentieth century with the Bauhaus design. Imperfection became associated with poor quality and kitsch.[9] As a consequence of the division of labour, the sites of production and sales were separated. Around 150 years ago, the first versions of the department store and shopping mall opened their doors.[10] The department stores did not, however, affect luxury immediately, as manufacturing remained a family business in the original store. This would not change until 1960.

2.1.2 A New Interpretation of Luxury Consumption

The Democratisation of Luxury

The democratisation of luxury started around 1960 and represents an ongoing process to make luxury goods and services available to a broader (and younger) audience. The biggest challenge was to avoid brand dilution because the idea of luxury is based on the inequality between aspirants to and customers of luxury goods. Exclusivity is a consequence rooted in contradictions: many people dream of a brand, but only a few can afford to buy an item from it. Making luxury available to new target groups implied the extension of custom-made high-end jewellery or watchmaking, as well as aspirational, high-end collections, towards affordable entry collections. Brand or line extensions were strategies to satisfy the need for affordable luxury.

- *Brand extension*: Montblanc is an excellent sample of brand extension. The German luxury brand was founded in 1906 and became famous for its exclusive writing instruments. Over time, Montblanc extended its brand to include new product categories, such as leather goods, jewellery, timepieces and even technical products, for instance smart watches and augmented paper.
- *Line extension*: Pomellato's Argento collection in sterling silver, Cartier's Tank watch in stainless steel and Tiffany's engagement ring are examples of line extension, as the product focus remains within the brand's core area of expertise: jewellery. There is always a certain risk of diluting the core brand

with line extensions, so luxury brands undertake such actions carefully. However, in high-end Italian fashion houses like Armani, it became common practice to create sub-labels under the flagship brand to offer different price ranges.

Further key factors reinforcing the positive modern perception of luxury include:

- Romantic consumerism
- Globalisation of luxury
- Digitalisation of luxury

Romantic Consumerism
Besides the creation of entry collections, the most important enabler of the democratisation of luxury was increased spending power, thanks to economic stability and peace. People had time and money to spend, and they no longer felt guilty about enjoying luxury. Consumption became an accepted manner of self-reward. We refer to this new way of thinking as romantic consumerism.[11] The romantic aspect motivates the exploitation of human potential through confrontation with the maximum multi-sensorial experience, while consumerism also creates the desire to try and consume as much as possible to be happy. The merging of the two aspects has created grateful luxury consumers.

The Globalisation of Luxury
Globalisation has also enabled growth. It started small, with brands like Gucci, which started exporting luxury goods in 1930.[12] The concept of having one store for one brand was then disrupted by the opening of new branches and mono-brand stores in vibrant metropolises throughout the world. Starting in 1980, the next phase began with the scaling up of the franchise system.[13]

At the time, most brands were run as family brands. The most recent phase, over the subsequent 20 years, was strongly characterised by the consolidation of luxury brands into conglomerates and private equity funds. In 1963, Francois Pinault set the first stone in the foundation of the PPR conglomerate (which became Kering in 2013). In 1987, Bernard Arnault took control of LVMH, followed one year later by the Rupert family's takeover of the Richemont Group. The advantages of those consolidations were linked to strategic group investments that provided scalability and synergy effects. The three biggest luxury conglomerates today are LVMH, Kering and Richemont, while the watch industry has been dominated by the Richemont Group, the

SWATCH Group and Rolex SA. The most famous independent brands in the context are Patek Philippe, Breitling, Chopard and Audemars Piguet, among others. Since 2000, the strategic creation of subsidiaries in priority markets and joint ventures has accelerated their international growth significantly. Conglomerates have played an important role in that evolution.

The Digitalisation of Luxury

As part of the expansion growth strategy, the online channel has gained increasing relevance. Despite luxury's cautious first steps towards digital, online sales and marketing rapidly became a core component of the future of luxury. In 2000, Net-a-Porter went live; in 2001, Vente-Privée.com opened its virtual doors; and in 2007, Farfetch was created. Thus far, the landscape of digital players and luxury conglomerates appeared to be clear and simple, but with the rise of new business models, the complexity would increase. This evolution also affected retail and wholesale channels when department stores themselves merged or were declared insolvent.

Deep Dive: Western Luxury Brands in Asia

Asia's shared history with Western luxury brands started at the end of the nineteenth century, when the first brands started to export luxury goods. Japan began trading jewellery with Europe, and Jacques Cartier travelled to India for the first time in 1911 to develop relationships with the Maharajas, who showed a strong passion for jewels. In around 1920, Shanghainese gentlemen in China started to enjoy wearing Omega and other Swiss timepieces, and the city was given its second name—the 'Paris of the East'.[14] Those convergences ended abruptly when the Second World War broke out.

After the war, luxury brands faced protective taxation policies in Asian countries, which made imports expensive. Those regulations still exist, in part, today. The average spending power of Asian countries has changed, however, and this has allowed the upper class and an increasing middle class to consume luxury goods.

Japan is now a mature luxury market, and Japanese citizens have become used to luxury. The consumption of luxury goods has also become standardised and predictable due to the strong hierarchical social structure in Japan. A certain status in society implies the ownership of certain branded goods. According to that logic, buying a Louis Vuitton bag in Japan is not optional if one wants to belong to a particular social set.

China, in contrast, follows the 'nouveaux riches' fashion, whereby people show off with Western items, and the difference between a luxury and a fashion brand is somewhat fluid to Chinese customers. People visualise what they want to achieve in life, and there is a special pleasure in picturing a world that contrasts with the monotone lifestyle cultivated during the restrictions of communism. China has, in the meantime, become more liberal in terms of fashion and luxury. Buying Western brands provides a way to express a type of identity that people lacked for a certain amount of time in history. Moving forward, Chinese people are about to reinvent their roots and culture through the creation of local luxury brands, such as LaoFengXiang, Qeelin, Zhaoyi Jade and Luk Fook.[15]

India has accepted Western luxury slowly due to its strong preference for local products. This preference is linked to the excellent work of Indian artisans as well as the country's declared independence. Manufacturing excellence was thus not a convincing reason to turn to Western brands because such products can be found with the same or higher quality locally. In particular, jewellery is traditionally bought based on material weight rather than brand name. For international luxury brands, there is only one approach to gain relevance: to blend into the local culture and traditions. What could be more suitable than launching collaborations with Bollywood? This was a strategy that yielded results for Omega, TAG Heuer and Rolex,[16] which became associated with appreciated industrial design instead of hand-made luxury.

2.2 Luxury and Consumer Goods: The Main Differentiation

Before the democratisation of luxury, it was easy to identify luxury. In alignment with the rapid transformation, the world has become more complex. In addition to true luxury brands, fashion, premium and masstige brands have started to offer watches and jewellery at affordable prices. However, high-end luxury and mass consumption can be differentiated from each other based on the following characteristics:

- Perceived scarcity
- High-end quality
- Symbolism
- Aesthetics
- Uniqueness
- High-end price

Perceived Scarcity

Perceived scarcity is an essential characteristic of luxury because it is based on a human truth: human desire increases in proportion to the limitations experienced in achieving or acquiring the desired good. In psychology, this is called the labour-love effect—that is, our appreciation for a product grows when we need to expend extra effort before calling it our own.[17] For instance, that effort translates into extra waiting time for the customer in cases of limited product availability. Another example of such extra investment builds the active involvement of the customer in the product configuration process to receive a unique personalised item for reward—in other words, an even more exclusive product. It does not matter whether the scarcity is real or artificially designed so long as the perceived emotion hits the target. Nevertheless, true luxury is based on real scarcity, while the masstige strategy allows artificially limited editions.[18] Scarcity as a core aspect of luxury implies conscious consumption and is therefore a natural promoter of sustainability.

High-End Quality

In comparison with soft luxury goods, the value of high-end jewellery and watches remains strongly connected with exclusive raw materials, such as gold, platinum or diamonds, even though new innovative materials, like ceramics, titanium or glass fibre, are entering the market. The applied material quality is a dominant differentiator in luxury. Gold, for example, is a limited resource. The only way to reduce the consumed raw material while keeping the look and feel is to use a less expensive alloy or to platinise a non-precious metal. The quality and price decrease as a consequence. Manufacturing has become partially automated thanks to modern foundry technology and CNC (computerised numerical control) metal processing. The assembly of complicated mechanical timepieces remains highly manual work. For timepieces, the complex and time-intense manufacturing of a mechanical or automatic movement with a variety of possible complications is a key quality differentiator in contrast to the significantly cheaper quartz movement.

Symbolism

Rolex enthusiasts give the impression that the symbolic value of a Rolex watch extends far beyond the functional utility of the time display—and this does not even begin to address the symbolism of rings and diamonds for a woman. The symbolism of luxury goods is an emotional driver, visibly highlighting a successful lifestyle to oneself and to others. Logos, 'Made in …' labels and hallmarks guarantee the high-quality origin and authenticity of a product. The booming counterfeit market copying luxury goods with all of the necessary love of detail shows that this is not the full truth in our modern world, but it emphasises the strong desire for luxury goods and the need to scale unique counterfeit-proof identifiers. Blockchain, radio-frequency identification (RFID), near-field communication (NFC) and Bluetooth technologies are brands' best friends in this fight for authenticity.

Aesthetics
Following the rules of art during creation leads to artwork in its finished status. The art of watchmaking and the art of fine jewellery build in references to the aesthetics of timeless products. Many brands have made art and timelessness a central part of their brand communication, as the following slogans show: 'A diamond is forever' (De Beers, jewellery, 1940), 'The art of being unique' (Cartier, jewellery, 1988), 'Eternal values' (Bulgari Octo, jewellery, 2013), 'Always around her' (Tiffany, jewellery, 2000), and 'Inspired by the past, built for the future' (Officine Panerai, watches, 2006).[19] Another parallel between luxury and art is the personality of the founder or designer, which is often presented in terms of being an artist. In fashion, the offer finds the customer, while in luxury, the customer finds the artist. In fashion, functionality is a requirement; in luxury, it is a nice thing to have. In fashion, unique aesthetics are nice to have, but in luxury, they are a requirement.

Uniqueness
The extraordinariness of luxury is the result of the combination of high-end quality materials with an innovative, sometimes provocative manner and unique design aesthetics as well as differentiating storytelling to realise extraordinary price points. Differentiating storytelling happens on the product or collection level but also on the brand level. Uniqueness at the product or collection level can be achieved through innovative manufacturing, such as Ross Lovegrove's 3D printed rings in 18-carat gold.[20] Uniqueness at the brand level often relates to the brand myth. The luxury myth typically refers to its elite customers, unique manufacturing techniques and long brand history. When a brand history is absent, it is usually invented through the conscious referencing of deliberately archaising elements, such as black-and-white images to give the brand image a historical colouring.

High-End Price

The luxury pricing strategy contrasts with that in other segments, like masstige. While most brands reduce their prices to increase the demand,[21] real luxury increases prices strategically and still tracks a positive impact on the customer demand. This effect is unique to luxury and was first identified by Thorstein Veblen.[22] Price elasticity is rooted in the common perception of luxury products as investments in the future.[23] The expectation concerning luxury items is that the timepiece or jewellery will last for a lifetime and even beyond. The watchmaker Patek Philippe successfully puts that legacy aspect at the centre of the brand's promise: 'You never actually own a Patek Philippe. You merely look after it for the next generation.' In an extension of the luxury pricing strategy, it is interesting to note that the Veblen effect is consciously applied to collaborations between luxury brands to raise prices and gain customers.[24] This is obvious when one considers timepiece models for racing car drivers, such as the 'Hublot Big Bang Ferrari Unico' or 'Classic Fusion Ferrari GT', 'Roger Dubuis Excalibur Aventador S' and 'Huracán' or 'Breitling's Premier B01 Chronograph 42 Bentley Centenary' and 'Mulliner'. Indeed, price reductions risk strongly diluting the perceived brand value.

2.3 Emotional Value Is the Key

People will forget what you said, people will forget what you did, but people will never forget how you made them feel.
—Maya Angelou, American Author

Luxury sells dreams. Luxury sells emotions—in other words, people desire luxury because it makes them feel good due to the positive emotions of self-esteem, status and respect of and by others. In Maslow's pyramid of needs, introduced in 1943, luxury in its extrinsic sense refers to the level of esteem (Fig. 2.1). Still, it is increasingly evolving into the top tier of self-actualisation and realisation, which is clearly intrinsically motivated. Think about product personalisation as a way to involve the creative customer actively in the product creation process as well as the evolution towards the experience of luxury and sustainability expectations of the LOHAS group.[25]

Nowadays, individuals are confronted by an average of 3000 advertising messages per day. Luxury brands accelerate decision-making processes by providing orientation: the best quality is a safe choice. In brain research, this phenomenon is called cortical relief[26]: the consumer stores a relevant brand set for certain product categories. Choosing the number one brand requires

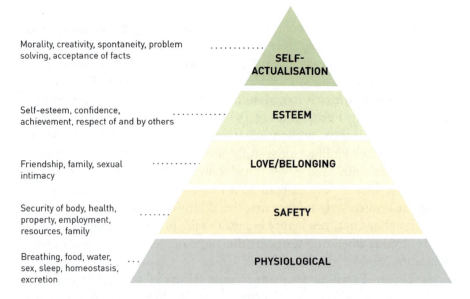

Fig. 2.1 Maslow's pyramid of needs (Adapted from Maslow, 1943)

less brain activity than choosing the second-favourite brand. The choice of the number one brand thus has a relieving effect, which corresponds to the fact that the decision is made not rationally but emotionally. Emotions are, so to speak, shortcuts for making quick decisions. The neuro-marketing scientist Dr Hans-Georg Häusel, father of the Limbic® map model, goes so far as to say that anything that does not trigger an emotion is worthless to the brain. He refers to the fact that 70 to 80 per cent of our decisions are taken unconsciously, based on emotions.[27] The limbic map illustrates the three key drivers: balance, stimulation and dominance. The last key driver translates into the most common driver of luxury brands, but the value mix varies among watchmakers and jewellery brands. A major benefit for luxury brands is to be emotionally charged at the pole position in the customer's mind.

2.3.1 Extrinsic Added Value

> *I don't wear a Tank to tell the time … I wear a Tank because it is the watch to wear!*
> —Andy Warhol, American Artist

Status is the perception of superiority. In different dimensions, it appears as a consequence of intellect, power, money or influence. The basic logic behind status is that it is granted typically by people who have already achieved superior status in a society—that is, the elites. The extrinsic added value of luxury is strongly linked to the visualisation of superiority, personality and social status through the consumption experience of high-end products and services. Two approaches have been studied in sociology. In 1899, Thorstein Veblen introduced the idea of conspicuous consumption within the theory of the leisure class, which was updated in 1979 when French philosopher Pierre Bourdieu published his theory on distinction.[28] While Veblen emphasised luxury as a socio-cultural code to be decoded by everyone within a certain society, Bourdieu extended that definition towards the freedom of an individual to distinguish himself or herself through consumption within that society. Following that interpretation, luxury should be exclusive, rare and innovative as it tends to lose its distinctive value when it becomes easily accessible for a broad audience.

Jewellery and watches are products that appear with internal and external spheres, but the pleasure of conspicuous consumption is particularly strong when wearing unique pieces in public or on stage. For example, in China, the engagement ring and the size of a diamond matter most to a woman's family as they represent the appreciation of and love for that specific woman. With the exception of India, buying branded jewellery for engagement and marriage ceremonies is expected to satisfy this extrinsic need everywhere. Red-carpet events are deeply connected to fine jewellery and watches, and the Cannes Film Festival (e.g.) would not be the same without the glamour and cameras. It is no surprise that even Instagram and other social media platforms have been transformed into global stages for the happy few to present themselves and their hold on the sweet life. In the moment of sharing the trappings of wealth with people who still dream of becoming part of the happy few one day, they intensify their own perception of being special and unique.[29]

2.3.2 Intrinsic Added Value

Intrinsically motivating luxury consumption is linked to self-esteem and self-reward. Both are essential human drivers, as everyone needs, first of all, self-esteem and confidence as a reward for special achievements in life, such as marriage, birth, promotion and, sometimes, even a surprise. It is human nature to progress as stasis is an unnatural and unhealthy state. People are trained to expect rewards thanks to education and experience at home, school and work. Through experienced recognition and respect, we become confident by being useful and necessary in the world.[30]

Because intrinsic added value is so connected with individual perception, it is only logical that it requires luxury brands to open the personal dialogue with the customer's ego. It is that ego that resonates with the communicated values and emotions of the brand. It is also that ego that wishes to be beautiful, appreciated and successful.[31] It is a personal decision to go the extra mile in one's life and career to be able to afford a Patek Philippe Nautilus timepiece or a unique secret like Blancpain's 'Le Brassus Erotic Minute Repeater Carrousel' one day. Despite the assertive price of such timepieces, the price itself is secondary in the dialogue with the customer's ego, as such a luxury purchase is primarily about the customer's dream of and desire for a unique item that is associated with strong emotion. If you do not believe this, take a moment to think about your most important luxury purchase and the role of the price in that decision. You purchased the creation in the end, right?

2.4 In Modern Life, Luxury Is Defined as an Experience

Those who perceive luxury as normal do not experience luxury.
—Lambert Wiesing, German Philosopher

We have seen how luxury has evolved dynamically over time and is differentiated from mass-consumer goods. Extrinsic and intrinsic motivation build the emotional core of human relationships with luxury brands and fine jewellery and timepieces. As illustrated by Lambert Wiesing's quote at the beginning of this chapter,[32] luxury is about the experience, and that is the definition that we will follow within this book.

After industrialisation, product functionality was perfected, and the emotional and experiential dimension is now the focus. The luxury understanding has thus moved from material towards immaterial luxury: towards experiences that money cannot buy. Examples of this include the wish to spend more quality time with family and friends or the personal value of being invited to 'Le Festival de Cannes' red-carpet event—the type of exclusive event that you cannot buy tickets for because the only way to become part of the club is to receive a personal invitation.

Luxury brands need to prioritise the omni-personal customer experience perception in their brand strategy. Innovations in production and information technologies, like 3D printing, artificial intelligence, big data management, virtual reality, connected objects or cloud computing, are fundamentally revolutionising society. Customers and their need for self-realisation need to be addressed along the value chain. This implies that customers would like to be welcomed personally across online and offline touchpoints. Customers are interested in becoming actively involved in the product configuration, which should take place through an engaging and rewarding approach. During that co-creation experience, the brand keeps control over the iconic product characteristics, while the customer adjusts colours and style facets within a predefined framework.

All marketing communication should consistently match the interest of individuals, considering their sales history and preferences. Customers should thus be able to control the communication channel through which they interact with a luxury brand, to select the experience and to switch seamlessly between online and offline touchpoints. One constraint in the consistency across channels and touchpoints is that, despite the use of digital autonomous sensory meridian response (ASMR) stimuli, it remains challenging to translate multi-sensory experiences into the digital world. Although visual and auditory impressions are realised, olfactory, tactile or taste impressions are currently still at the starting stage, facing limitations.

Beyond the focus on holistic experience in the luxury market, it is also important to notice that brands take over essential social and transcendent functions that in the past have been covered by religion. Well-loved brands intend to provide orientation and spiritual meaning to individuals. Thanks to their strength in storytelling, they know how to update the brand myth continuously for their followers, while flagship stores act as modern temples. Kapferer describes this as follows:

> *Consumers visit the stores in small groups, as in a pilgrimage, and wish to attend the rituals delivered there on a one-to-one basis (welcoming, services, mode of address, demonstration, explanation of the exceptionality of each item, etc.). This comparison with religion is most revealing: luxury likes to present itself as an elevating cultural force.*[33]

Iconic products are presented in a ritualised and personal way. Through that ritual experience, human-made objects obtain a spiritual meaning that builds on immaterial values and corresponds to the human need for transcendence. When luxury brands refer to the active management of brand equity, they actually link to the active management of the brand myth based on strategic storytelling and the updating of brand icons. Building a relationship with a luxury brand as an external customer—and even as an internal employee—implies committing to the brand myth and religion because that is the only way to update a brand through unique, immaterial and differentiating experiences. In that context, Alfred Adler's strength of personality model is also true for brands[34]: the strength of a brand is the outcome of the perfect balance between:

- The internal perception of the brand
- The external market perception
- The way in which the brand wants to be perceived

Luxury brands need to harmonise all three levels to strengthen the brand experience for their internal and external stakeholders.

Notes

1. Danziger P (2019) Meet the HENRYS: the millennials that matter most for luxury. Paramount Market Publishing, Ithaca, p 19.
2. Cappellieri A, Tenuta L (2020) Jewellery between product and experience: luxury in the twenty-first century. In: Gardetti MÁ, Coste-Manière I (eds) Sustainable luxury and craftsmanship: environmental footprints and eco-design of products and processes. Springer Nature Singapore Pte Ltd, Singapore, pp 1–23.
3. Cartier Brickell, F (2019) The Cartiers: the untold story of the family behind the jewellery empire. Random House, New York, p 584.
4. Kapferer J (2015) Kapferer on luxury: how luxury brands can grow yet remain rare. Kogan Page, London, p 99.
5. Kapferer J, Bastien V (eds) (2012) The luxury strategy: break the rules of marketing to build luxury brands. Kogan Page, London, p 16.
6. Chevalier M, Gutsatz M (eds) (2019) Luxury retail and digital management. Wiley, New Jersey, Location 844.
7. Pietzcker D (2018) Luxus jenseits ideologischer Kritik und affirmativer Haltungen. In: Pietzcker D, Vaih-Baur C (eds) Luxus als Distinktionsstrategie: Kommunikation in der internationalen Luxus- und Fashionindustrie. Springer, Wiesbaden, pp 3–19.
8. Cartier Brickell, F (2019) The Cartiers: the untold story of the family behind the jewellery empire. Random House, New York, p 389.
9. Barta S, Stoklossa U (2018) Without design, it's just a lump of gold—future developments in design as luxury. In: Pietzcker D, Vaih-Baur C (eds) Luxus als Distinktionsstrategie: Kommunikation in der internationalen Luxus- und Fashionindustrie. Springer, Wiesbaden, pp 83–94.
10. Chevalier M, Gutsatz M (eds) (2019) Luxury retail and digital management. Wiley, New Jersey, Location 875.

11. Harari Y (2013) Eine kurze Geschichte der Menschheit. Deutsche Verlags-Anstalt, Munich, p 194.
12. Chadha R, Husband P (2006) The cult of the luxury brand: inside Asia's love affair with luxury. Nicholas Brealey International, London, p 517.
13. Chevalier M, Gutsatz M (eds) (2019) Luxury retail and digital management. Wiley, New Jersey, Location 1284.
14. Chadha R, Husband P (2006) The cult of the luxury brand: inside Asia's love affair with luxury. Nicholas Brealey International, London, p 27.
15. Doran S (2011) 11 fine jewellery designers, China & Taiwan. https://www.luxurysociety.com/en/articles/2011/11/11-fine-jewellery-designers-china-taiwan/. Accessed 25 November 2020.
16. Chadha R, Husband P (2006) The cult of the luxury brand: inside Asia's love affair with luxury. Nicholas Brealey International, London, pp 124, 426; Kapferer J, Bastien V (eds) (2012) The luxury strategy: break the rules of marketing to build luxury brands. Kogan Page, London, p 152.
17. Spreer P (2018) PsyConversion: 101 Behavior Patterns für eine bessere User Experience und höhere Conversion -Rate im E-Commerce. Springer, Wiesbaden, p 537.
18. Corbellini E, Saviolo S (2014) Managing fashion and luxury companies. Rizzoli Etas, Milan, p 191.
19. Slogans.de (2020) Slogans.de. https://www.slogans.de/slogans.php?GInput=cartier. Accessed 19 July 2020.
20. Caula R (2013) Ross Lovegrove 3D prints gold rings for Louisa Guinness Gallery. https://www.designboom.com/design/ross-lovegrove-3d-prints-18k-gold-rings-for-louisa-guinness-gallery-11-30-2013/. Accessed 30 November 2020.
21. Kapferer J, Bastien V (eds) (2012) The luxury strategy: break the rules of marketing to build luxury brands. Kogan Page, London, p 247.
22. Veblen T (1899) The theory of the leisure class. Oxford University Press, New York, p 76.
23. Webber J (2018) Luxury consumption, seen under a contemporary light. In: Pietzcker D, Vaih-Baur C (eds) Luxus als Distinktionsstrategie: Kommunikation in der internationalen Luxus- und Fashionindustrie. Springer, Wiesbaden, pp 83–94, 182.
24. Langer D, Heil O (2015) Luxury essentials: essential insights and strategies to manage luxury products. Center for Research on Luxury, Mainz, p 97.
25. Estève C (2016) Understanding luxury through Maslow's hierarchy of needs. https://www.agora.universite-paris-saclay.fr/understanding-luxury-through-maslows-hierarchy-of-needs/. Accessed 21 November 2020.
26. Scheier C, Held D (eds) (2012) Wie Werbung wirkt: Erkenntnisse des Neuromarketing. Haufe, Freiburg, pp 25, 34.
27. Häusel H (eds) (2016) Brain View: Warum Kunden kaufen. Haufe, Freiburg, p 27.

28. Bourdieu P (1985) A social critique of the judgement of taste. Harvard University Press, Cambridge.
29. Barta S, Stoklossa U (2018) Without design, it's just a lump of gold—future developments in design as luxury. In: Pietzcker D, Vaih-Baur C (eds) Luxus als Distinktionsstrategie: Kommunikation in der internationalen Luxus- und Fashionindustrie. Springer, Wiesbaden, p 629.
30. Maslow A (1943) A theory of human motivation. Psychol Rev 50: 370–396.
31. Srun F (2017) Luxury selling: lessons from the world of luxury in selling high quality goods and services to high value clients. Palgrave Macmillan, Hampshire, Locations 1256, 1797.
32. Wiesing L (eds) (2015) Luxus. Suhrkamp, Berlin.
33. Kapferer J (2015) Kapferer on luxury: how luxury brands can grow yet remain rare. Kogan Page, London, p 52.
34. Kunde J (2000) Corporate religion. Financial Times Prentice Hall, London, p 128.

3

Cautious Steps Towards Digital

Key Aspects

- In the past, the Internet experience and price focus did not match the needs of luxury.
- As the first step, luxury brands created a web presence based on a static offline marketing approach.
- As the second step, e-commerce business models evolved.
- The online channel was dominated by entry products, overstock and second-hand products.
- Besides mono-brand stores, pure digital players entered the market.
- Social media focused on brand awareness by emphasising product characteristics instead of accessibility.
- As part of giving customers their own voice, influencers play an essential role.
- Asian markets are mobile, open minded and early adopters of innovation.
- New trends like social commerce are now born in Asia, no longer in the United States.
- Social commerce itself is not new, but digital live shopping features allow a new level of personal brand experience.
- Today the ambivalence between luxury and the Internet is decreasing and the need for phygital is increasing.

Despite or because of its focus on exclusive in-store experiences and face-to-face customer relationships, luxury brands have not disrupted the digital world. Luxury brands have chosen a careful follower approach towards the digital world because the poor quality of the Internet appeared to be the industry's major challenge (besides the democratisation of luxury). The store remained the centre of the multi-sensory brand experience, while the Internet at first only offered basic 1.0 data visualisation made for another world and purpose. Technical innovation, usability and customer expectations have evolved radically since the invention of the World Wide Web.

3.1 The Fear of Brand Dilution Slowed Transformation

The initial relationship between luxury and the Internet describes 'the big search for differences': luxury is about culture, heritage, timelessness and rarity. Luxury is about controlled one-to-one relationships and exclusive communication. In contrast, the Internet is about accessibility, availability, usability and impermanence. The Internet stands for automatisation, mass communication, democracy and a certain lack of control. Luxury is about being small and exclusive, while digital is about being big. The Internet is also associated with tempting deals, open sources, offers for free goods, discounts or at least price transparency. For example, between 1999 and 2005, numerous shopping comparison sites were launched successfully, but luxury continued to mystify its pricing, which in part explains the ambivalence between luxury and the Internet (Fig. 3.1).

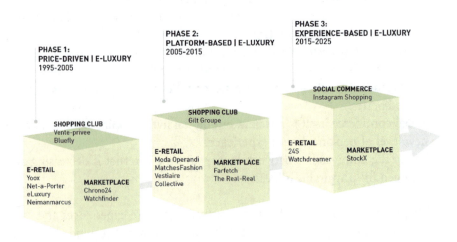

Fig. 3.1 Luxury and e-commerce—evolution in three phases, excluding Chinese platforms (see Sect. 3.2.2)

In short, the Internet did not match luxury's need for exclusivity. Moving online despite that knowledge would have created a clear risk of diluting the brand value. Therefore, the low maturity of the technology acted as a general reason or excuse to postpone brands' decision to show their face online. It ultimately became obvious, however, that the Internet was here to stay. Answering that, luxury brands created their first Internet presence, maintaining the golden rule that only the best was good enough. In contrast, Internet use explicitly focused on building the dream, just like any other marketing channel dedicated to driving brand awareness. However, selling the dream should remain an in-store experience. Better to be safe than sorry.

Digital luxury in the era of Web 1.0 was a static copy of offline marketing actions based on a website with sub-pages for the brand philosophy, history or static brochures. In that first phase, defining the strategic role for the new online channel was particularly important: following competitors, preventing competitors from increasing their market share, communicating with customers or simply providing basic company information, such as the address, operating hours and store locations.[1]

3.1.1 The Rise of e-Commerce Was Previously Price Driven

When luxury entered e-commerce around 2000, it happened carefully and selectively in terms of distribution channels and products. That is called 'the art of absence'.[2] As highlighted in Sect. 2.1.2 in Chap. 2, brand and line extensions are common strategies that luxury brands use to introduce affordable entry products and collections to the market. As those collections were designed for a broader, middle-class audience, they offered the most natural entry point to e-commerce. Brands started to sell online entry products and offered limited editions developed for the Web only. In parallel, Gucci, Hermés and Tiffany were among the first to launch mono-brand online shops.

In the context of fine jewellery and watches, the digital transformation made slow progress.[3] Entry tickets could still be a pretty expensive pleasure as they tended to be higher priced in jewellery and watches than in other personal luxury categories, such as leather goods and accessories. The personal link with the customer therefore remained a key driver of the in-store experience, which continued to be highly relevant in the luxury market. Even loyal customers kept the in-store ceremony as their preferred touchpoint for enjoying the facets of extraordinary pieces. There have always been exceptions to the rule, of course, so at present we can find creations worth US$300,000 or more sold online, even if this seldom happens. Although online sales platforms became convenient for premium and fashion brands, for luxury, they acted as a complementary channel to inform customers about the brand besides extending the customer service. Nevertheless, digital communication remained one directional (top down) to keep the circle of customers at a distance exclusively by preventing access to those who are still 'dreaming' of luxury.

The first purely digital luxury players opened their virtual doors with multi-brand platforms in 2000: London-based Net-a-Porter and Milan-based Yoox went live, closely followed by eLuxury (which belonged to LVMH until its closure in 2009 due to its failure to build a sufficiently strong brand to withstand the competition). At that time, online sales accounted for around 2 per cent of the overall personal luxury consumption.[4]

Deep Dive: Yoox—From Discount e-Retail to Market Disruptor

The business model for online-only luxury sales sites actively promoted discounts, particularly in the case of Yoox or Bluefly. These platforms exclusively sold overstock from previous seasons with significant discounts. The offerings were naturally limited by the product availability of former collections. Luxury brands solely focusing on jewellery and watches did not sell via discount e-retailers, but for fashion, it was a method to keep distribution channels separate. In an ideal luxury world, sales campaigns should never happen at all, but if they cannot be avoided, they should definitely not be carried out in the mono-brand online shop, side by side with the full-priced new collection. Luxury and e-commerce were not looking for each other, but they were a match made in heaven for selling out-dated collections.

Over time, Yoox said goodbye to the discount business model and created unique benefits for its customers through design expertise and collaborations with young, innovative designers. With growing fashion expertise and strategic restructuring, Yoox built the foundation to evolve into a luxury ecosystem, offering brands white-label services, including e-commerce software, a design studio and RFID technology. Yoox and Kering created a joint venture in 2010 before Yoox purchased Net-a-Porter shares in 2015 and Richemont acquired 95 per cent of the Yoox-Net-a-Porter (YNAP) shares in 2018. To date, Yoox keeps its fashion focus in alignment with its Italian soul, while beyond fashion, Net-a-Porter also showcases jewellery and watch brands.

In parallel to the launch of mono-brand online shops, department stores and retailers like Neiman Marcus, MatchesFashion, Printemps and Galeries

Lafayette were inspired by the tremendous success of technology giants such as Amazon, Apple and Google. These retail chains launched their own e-commerce sites, and the Neiman Marcus Group started to offer white-label services to selected brands. Whether they involved limited-entry product collections for mono- and multi-brand stores, shopping clubs or marketplaces, all of these first steps into the digital world considered the customers' price sensitivity.

3.1.2 E-commerce Meets Luxury in Shopping Clubs

The main characteristic of shopping clubs was scarcity, based on limited-time offers (over only a few days) and limited product availability, accessible only to members of the shopping club. The combination resulted in tempting price discounts of up to 70 per cent off the original price point and, more importantly, a strong desire to buy quickly. The business model showed that the lesson in digital flash sales à la Amazon had been learned. As in the case of discount e-retailers, the products came from previous collection overstock. Since 2002, shopping clubs like Vente-Privée, Gilt and BuyVIP have kicked off as a sub-category on multi-brand e-retailer platforms.

The fear of brand dilution remained the biggest risk to this business model, while certain Web 2.0 features were integrated to protect the exclusiveness of the platform. In the case of Vente-Privée, a recommendation from a current member was needed to become part of the club and to place an order. Due to such social elements, shopping clubs act as the first digital example of social commerce. For pure jewellery and watch brands, like Chaumet and Breguet, shopping clubs have never played a leading role. For fashion brands, they remain relevant today, even though they are increasingly becoming obsolete. For the likes of white-label solutions like that of Farfetch or YNAP, Vente-Privée offers an interesting option for internal staff sales within brands and conglomerates.

3.1.3 Second-Hand Marketplaces Sell an Affordable Dream

Another way to make the dream of fine jewellery or timepieces affordable is to buy vintage products via second-hand marketplace platforms such as eBay or other specialised platforms.

Global Second-Hand Marketplaces
At the beginning of online second-hand luxury, there was only eBay, founded in 1995. Transactions on eBay stand for a business of trust between buyer and seller. Unfortunately, eBay became extremely popular among counterfeiters for selling Rolex, Patek Philippe and other fraudulent products, which is now being tackled with the help of its own authentication tool.

Specialised Second-Hand Marketplaces (for Jewellery and Watches)
Buying on specialised platforms provided a higher level of service and security than marketplaces like eBay. Specialised platforms provided additional buyer protection, authenticity certification and guarantee services. Moreover, specialists checked the vendor identity and transaction history and offered filters and facets to enhance usability. For luxury second-hand marketplaces dedicated to watches, we can mention Watchfinder, founded in 2002, and Chrono24, founded in 2003. Both platforms offer additional features for watch connoisseurs, such as the virtual try-on feature of Chrono24 or the product comparison tool of Watchfinder. It is interesting to note that around one-third of the second-hand watches sold via Chrono24 are Rolex models.[5]

With specialised luxury platforms, such as Vestiaire Collective, founded in 2009, or the RealReal, founded in 2011, sustainability and the circular economy have become the focus. The new emphasis on sustainability is remarkable as initially second-hand items were sold primarily via the strong price argument. Still, younger generations continue to push for socially, economically and environmentally responsible production and consumption. In consequence, the ownership value of luxury is shifting in the sense that the luxury experience is becoming more important. That experience can also be attained through luxury resale or rental models. According to a market research study conducted by Altiant in mature second-hand markets like the United States, the United Kingdom and France, 84 per cent, the majority of respondents, did not link any stigma to second-hand luxury goods.[6] The global market for second-hand luxury goods increased from €17 billion in 2015 to €26 billion in 2019.[7]

3.1.4 The Ambivalent Relationship of Luxury and e-Commerce

Due to the Internet's focus on price transparency and discounts, alignment with a high-end luxury strategy remained challenging because of the fear of brand dilution and financial losses. While certain luxury brands managed to make entry products accessible to a broad audience, they completely avoided shopping clubs. They watched second-hand platforms like eBay with a sceptical eye. This caused them to return to the point at which a luxury strategy calls for maximum control, especially in the online context, in which absolute control is impossible by default.[8] Jewellery and watch brands like Tiffany, Bulgari, Cartier and Rolex have therefore developed mono-brand online shops while establishing exclusive partnerships and joint ventures with e-retailers. For smaller brands, collaboration with e-retailers and their white-label services often becomes a reasonable solution. Certainly, when a brand decides to sell online, it is generally likely to create a web presence on multiple platforms to increase the potential for touchpoints and sales.[9]

However, the market dynamics and acquisitions in the last years have encouraged conglomerates to stay flexible and autonomous. Richemont's acquisition of YNAP in 2018 constituted one of those events as Yoox had previously partnered closely with Kering. While YNAP was in charge of the logistics and technology platform, Kering controlled the brand's online shops, assorted editorial content and communication.[10] After the acquisition, Kering started to move forward independently. Brands and conglomerates have a fair interest in this kind of control and flexibility at any time.

Customers are also now browsing for more than just the best price. Inspiration, entertainment, education and conscious consumption have become much more important, as we have seen with the latest generation of specialised second-hand luxury platforms. The Internet has also allowed the development of completely new business models, such as Farfetch, which was founded by José Neves in 2008.

Deep Dive: Farfetch—A Digital Marketplace for Multi-brand Stores

Farfetch is based on the idea of simplifying communication between global luxury customers and multi-brand stores on a common marketplace platform. The customer database and online expertise of each individual store were not sufficiently mature, so scalability effects at the single-store level appeared to be impossible. Farfetch merged forces via its online platform to scale the business and synergies. In return, it coordinated merchandising aligned with luxury principles and charged a commission on each item sold, while the store remained responsible for shipment. In other words, Farfetch enabled the ship-from-store scenario for external stores. In contrast to shopping clubs or second-hand marketplaces, the business model did not differentiate through price and was not limited to an audience of registered members. The added value for the customer was linked to the experience and product accessibility of extraordinary pieces.

Since 2015, the platform has launched its brand shops as well as the black-and-white service to allow brands to develop their mono-brand e-commerce solution based on the Farfetch stack. Farfetch has, as a consequence, evolved into a platform for mono-brand and multi-brand sales with the mission to connect creators, curators and customers, acting as a global platform for luxury fashion. Even though the Farfetch marketplace model was different from the e-retail model of YNAP, both platforms grew into ecosystems that surround brands with omni-channel software and services. This gave an advantage to those that maintained a strategic partnership with YNAP or Farfetch, which was realised (notably) by Richemont and Kering but also by independent brands like Chanel, which have invested in Farfetch. In 2020, Alibaba teamed up with Richemont to invest US$1.1 billion in Farfetch, with a focus on China.

To sum up, the ambivalence between luxury brands and the Internet is decreasing, and it is obvious that there is no way forward for one without the other. Today, the online share of the personal luxury market is roughly 10 per cent. In 2018, that represented around €28 billion in online sales.[11] For luxury, this translates into a clear focus on omni-personal phygital experiences, which means answering the question of how to blend online and offline to gain the best of both worlds. Luxury is facing a unifying trend towards one omni-channel world and one omni-personal experience.

3.2 Social Media: The Entry and Extension Area to Drive Brand Growth

Luxury is a social marker, so luxury on social media is not as strange as it initially appeared in 2007. Still, as the expression and symbol of the democratic voice of a digital revolution, luxury brands resisted entering the digital dialogue with their fans and followers. In the end, however, the visual and social power of social networks convinced the stakeholders involved. The voice of the customer matters. As an awareness channel, social media created the perfect match to emphasise products' characteristics—not their accessibility.

Social media's rapid growth is explained by the rise of mobile devices and user engagement that is achieved through interactive communication and relationship building. From liking and following, through sharing and commenting to messages, all social media interactions aim to personalise the customer–brand relationship and give customers the positive feeling of belonging to an exclusive brand community.[12] This is equally true for Facebook, Twitter, Instagram, Snapchat, WeChat, Weibo and TikTok and, in 2018, resulted in a total of 1.04 billion tracked social engagement actions in the luxury domain.[13] Increasingly, the initial luxury approach seen on social media is extending towards phygital product interactions, commerce and the integration of analytics and CRM for customer segmentation and clienteling.

3.2.1 Influencers Cultivate Brand Glam on Social Networks

We should not forget, in the social media context, that the origin of social media lies in people's need to make their digital interactions more social and interactive. Open diaries inspired the first blogs and became a kind of self-expression for members of Gen Y, allowing them to share their opinions about specific interests, the world and, at a certain point, brands and products. The core of social media builds on people—that is, young people who live and experience brands like family members or beloved persons become brand ambassadors and finally influencers or key opinion leaders (KOLs) when they start to share their perceptions, feelings and recommendations online.

First, the open-source content-management system WordPress and blog service Blogger have smoothed the path for independent blogs. Second, Facebook, Twitter, YouTube and Instagram have built their platforms on the network idea. Third, the content has moved from picture to video and from video to virtual life experience, as we can see on platforms like Snapchat, Instagram, Periscope and TikTok. Regarding the number of users, Facebook remains the leading network, with 2.45 billion users globally in 2020, followed by YouTube, with 2 billion, and Instagram, with 1 billion.[14]

All of these platforms give people and thoughts a virtual home and sense of belonging to a community that is accessible whenever and wherever needed via a mobile phone, which fits into a pocket. Thanks to smartphones, a camera to capture 'best-of' moments is always present. This has led to the initially paid role of VIP testimonials being extended towards normal people with an over-proportional passion for and expertise in brands. Why? The answer is simple and straightforward: trust. Authentic people and customers with a real passion are by nature the best brand ambassadors for the following reasons:

- *Engagement*: They know the brand from their own experience and happily engage with it in the role of a confident customer, critical reviewer or coaching expert for products that need explanation.
- *Content production*: They are not ashamed to show off with user-generated content. For instance, countless selfies underline the unlimited combination possibilities of a piece of jewellery.
- *Brand awareness*: They use their reach to spread the word and trigger the bandwagon effect through, for example, posts promoting offers, contests and events appearing next to news about family and friends on the user timeline.
- *Customer-relevant products*: They act as sounding boards for existing products and campaigns, but beyond that, they become involved in creating and testing future collections to share their customer perspective.

With the rise of Gen Z, the role of influencers is changing again as they are no longer seen as independent opinion leaders. Influencer marketing has emerged as an official marketing type, and it is an open secret that influencers are compensated by brands in different ways. With increasing professionalisation, social media influencers are losing trust and credibility for upcoming generations like Gen Z. However, the need for social networks is still immense, and the virtual dialogue begins for some before they even learn to speak.

3.2.2 Chinese Social Media Affinity Opens New Doors for Social Commerce

While it was a rarity in Europe until a few years ago to see a toddler playing with an iPad or Daddy's mobile phone, in China and other Asian countries, this has not been a curiosity for quite some time. First, in China, 98 per cent of Internet users are mobile users. Second, as a highly collectivist culture, China differentiates between in- and out-groups. This means that social media platforms have enormous importance because they promote a sense of community. Accordingly, it is only logical that Chinese people spend an average of two hours daily on Chinese social media platforms to strengthen their in-group positioning. Their preferred platforms are WeChat (1.2 billion users), TikTok (0.8 billion users), QQ, Sina Weibo and Youku.[15] The platform landscape in China looks different from that in the rest of the world due to restricted web access (Fig. 3.2). Chinese mirror platforms have replaced Western platforms, which are censored in the Chinese market.

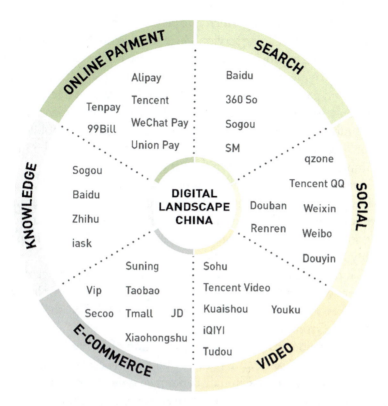

Fig. 3.2 The digital platform landscape in China

Asians were early adopters and were more open minded and positivistic about technical innovations. This affected privacy but ultimately led to a more playful approach towards interacting with the new digital world. Many new tech, commerce and logistic companies have been founded in China over the last years. The two giants, Alibaba and JD, have constantly developed their ecosystems to provide new retail services for their customers. Their hunger for growth and innovation made these companies huge. Today, they set international trends that are born in Asia, rather than in the United States. The latest trends are live streaming and social commerce, strategic use of shopping coupons and gift cards and even the introduction of new shopping holidays, like JD's founding date of 18 June and 'Singles' Day' on the symbolic double one date of 11.11—and yes, the 1 stands for single!

Social media are moving from awareness driving to sales, referred to as 'social commerce'. The most popular social media platforms enabling live streaming and commerce in China are the following:

- *WeChat (Weixin)*: Tencent, which also holds shares in JD.com, developed the social instant messaging service WeChat. In recent years, it has emerged as an ecosystem that provides a wide range of services, including e-commerce storefronts, payment gateways, customer service, broadcasts, mini programmes and games. A total of 1.2 billion active users interact monthly via Weixin and its English version WeChat. In particular, e-commerce has become more important, as 36 per cent of users open the mobile application for shopping versus 31 per cent for customer service and 33 per cent for company, event or product information.[16]
- *TikTok (Douyin)*: Douyin, and its international version, TikTok, is a young and fast-growing social media application based on live streaming and short videos, with 400 million monthly active users.[17] Due to its focus on KOLs and brands and its dominant engagement with Gen Z, the platform is highly relevant for luxury brands.
- *QQ*: The penguin logo stands for an instant messaging service developed by Tencent offering social games, microblogging, music, shopping and further services to 647 million active users monthly.[18] The social networks Penyou and Qzone also belong to QQ.
- *Sina Weibo*: Weibo is the Chinese interpretation of Twitter's microblogging service and, in that sense, is a platform that allows brands to post news to stay up to date and to disseminate content at scale. Alibaba has invested in Weibo and, hence, full integration with Alipay is targeted. Recently, Weibo launched an e-commerce extension, called Xiaodian ('little shop'), which enables users to manage inventory and transactions via a mini programme. However, the commission is higher than on competitors' platforms. It makes sense for luxury brands to build the Weibo channel around awareness while keeping the commerce transactions on brand-controlled commerce channels.[19] Weibo also supports seamless integration with the popular live-streaming provider Yizhibo. Besides the streaming service, the community is authorised to send virtual gifts in real time. During the COVID-19 lockdown, Yizhibo helped to turn empty luxury stores into virtual shopping stages, and sales associates took on the role of virtual hosts.
- *Little Red Book (Xiaohongshu)*: Originally a product review forum for high-end fashion and beauty for Chinese tourists travelling abroad, Little Red Book evolved into a social commerce platform for millennials and has 100 million monthly active users. The mobile application has a clear focus on international luxury goods, particularly for a female audience, so brands like Louis Vuitton have launched live-streaming features as part of their campaigns.

The most popular e-commerce platforms moving into live streaming and social commerce are the following:

- *Tmall and Taobao*: Taobao is a C2C commerce platform, which translates into China's eBay. Tmall, in contrast, concentrates on the B2C channel, which is sub-structured into Tmall Classic, Global, Luxury Pavilion and the new outlet format Soho. Both commerce hubs belong to Alibaba and generate over 800 million monthly active users, and both are sales driven when it comes to live streaming. The average conversion rate on content is 32 per cent.[20] It is no surprise that the Tmall Luxury Pavilion is the place to be for luxury brands, as is already the case for many luxury houses as well as the Watches & Wonders exhibition, which launched a live-streaming campaign on Tmall in collaboration with YNAP.
- *Secoo*: Secoo is an online marketplace for vintage and new luxury goods, extending into concierge services, such as hotel and travel reservations. It follows an omni-channel approach, including the opening of brick-and-mortar stores or white-glove delivery services. Due to the COVID-19 crisis, Secoo partnered with the video platform Kuaishou, which also maintains a strategic partnership with JD, to set up a 24-hour live-streaming event, including themed rooms hosted by different KOLs.[21] The success of that event potentially provides a starting point for something bigger in the future.

China is a big step ahead in terms of social commerce. While the rest of the world is still differentiating between social media for entertainment and e-commerce for shopping, in China the two have merged into social commerce. The perfect format seems to be live streaming, but that might change. While, in the rest of the world, Gen Z is starting to view influencers more cautiously, in China, a brand without KOLs will not succeed. As mentioned earlier, China is a collective society, caring strongly about the thoughts of family members and idols. The trusted personal relationship between influencers and followers will matter to ensure the permanent success of social commerce. In 2019, the value of social commerce in China was estimated to have reached US$300 billion with a rising trend.[22]

3.2.3 Social Commerce Conquers the World

Social commerce and e-commerce will be an area of focus for the years ahead. (…) With the internet came an abundance of information—and especially younger audiences look for curated content and product recommendations.
   —Kristian Tear, CEO of Bang & Olufsen, Questionnaire Conducted by the Authors

Social commerce is not completely new. Tupperware parties, shopping clubs and teleshopping acted as pioneering models. The transfer to an interactive virtual world is, however, definitely new. The fact that mobile phones enable customers to communicate in real time with the famous host of a live-streaming session creates new emotions. The tremendous success of social commerce in China is driven by collectivism and extraordinary experiences in a world where consumption defines one's identity. In countries without a post-communist catch-up, the success of social commerce may be more moderate. Still, due to the generation change—and accelerated by COVID-19—live streaming will certainly be an essential marketing component in the future.

International social media platforms, like Facebook and Instagram, have already launched social shopping tools. As the next step, Zuckerberg announced that live shopping features are being tested to allow the display of product pages during a live-streaming session.[23] YouTube and TikTok are well positioned to kick off advanced virtual live shopping as both platforms have their key expertise in real-time video streaming and entertainment. In contrast, Amazon is struggling with its live shopping channel. The 'Style Code Live' programme that it released in 2016 ended one year later. With 'Amazon Live', a new programme based on live product demonstration entered the market. The presented products are displayed below the video stream on a product carousel. Nevertheless, the new channel does not yet attract the same level of attention as competitors' solutions do. Important questions in the context of luxury and premium remain. Do you control the exclusiveness of social commerce events? How do you ensure a personal welcome ceremony? How do you position your brand's uniqueness? Should the audience of live shopping events be limited? Are sales associates the perfect live shopping hosts?

Notes

1. Okonkwo U. (2010) Luxury online: styles, systems, strategies. Palgrave Macmillan, Hampshire, p 148.
2. Kapferer J (2015) Kapferer on luxury: how luxury brands can grow yet remain rare. Kogan Page, London, p 32.
3. Canaves S (2020) Hard luxury gets the livestreaming treatment. https://jing-daily.com/hard-luxury-gets-the-livestreaming-treatment. Accessed 30 April 2020.
4. Sherman L (2020) The next wave of luxury e-commerce. In: The business of fashion. https://www.businessoffashion.com/education/courses/case-study-luxury-ecommerce-online-retail, p 4. Accessed 30 April 2020.

5. Lux T (2020) Wie in Karlsruhe mit Chrono24 der weltweit größte Marktplatz für Luxusuhren entstanden ist. https://omr.com/de/chrono24-tim-stracke-podcast/. Accessed 15 April 2020.
6. Altiant (2019) New models of luxury ownership: resale, rentals & subscriptions. https://altiant.com/new-models-of-luxury-ownership, p 9. Accessed 30 November 2020.
7. Sherman L (2020) The next wave of luxury e-commerce. In: The business of fashion. https://www.businessoffashion.com/education/courses/case-study-luxury-ecommerce-online-retail, p 7. Accessed 30 April 2020.
8. Abtan O, Barton C (2016) Digital or die: the choice for luxury brands. www.bcg.com/publications/2016/digital-or-die-choice-luxury-brands.aspx. Accessed 20 October 2020.
9. Chevalier M, Gutsatz M (eds) (2019) Luxury retail and digital management. Wiley, New Jersey, Location 2162.
10. Guiltbault L (2020) LVMH and Kering's new battlefield is online. https://www.voguebusiness.com/companies/lvmh-and-kerings-new-battlefield-is-online-covid-19. Accessed 12 June 2020.
11. Achille A (2019) McKinsey and Altagamma—win big in digital. Altagamma. https://altagamma.it/media/source/turtl-story-nAcnMU_1.pdf, p.11. Accessed 10 December 2020.
12. Bairamian H (2018) Les marques des produits de luxe face aux medias sociaux. https://nanopdf.com/download/les-marques-des-produits-de-luxe-face-aux-medias-sociaux_pdf, p 4. Accessed 26 January 2021.
13. Gartner (2019) Lessons from luxury retail—younger generation lead the way. https://www.gartner.com/en/documents/3905168/lessons-from-luxury-retail-younger-generations-lead-the-, p 7. Accessed 20 March.
14. Statista (2020) Ranking der größten Social Networks und Messenger nach der Anzahl der Nutzer im Januar 2020. https://de.statista.com/statistik/daten/studie/181086/umfrage/die-weltweit-groessten-social-networks-nach-anzahl-der-user/. Accessed 20 January 2021.
15. Dudarenok AG, Zakkour M (2019) New retail born in China going global: how Chinese tech giants are changing global commerce. Independently published, p 132; Statista (2020) Ranking der größten Social Networks und Messenger nach der Anzahl der Nutzer im Januar 2020. https://de.statista.com/statistik/daten/studie/181086/umfrage/die-weltweit-groessten-social-networks-nach-anzahl-der-user/. Accessed 20 January 2021.
16. Chang A, Mauron P (2020) JingDigital and Digital Luxury Group—WeChat luxury index 2020. JingDigital. https://www.jingdigital.com/en/articles/8255/, p 2, 50. Accessed 3 April 2021.
17. Jing Daily (2020) Next level livestreaming: how luxury brands can profit from China's top e-commerce trend. https://jingdaily.com/wp-content/uploads/2020/08/Next-Level-Luxury-Livestreaming-2020-Jing-Daily-CCI.pdf. Accessed 30 April 2020.

18. Statista (2020) Number of monthly active smart device users of Tencent QQ in China from 2014 to 2019. https://www.statista.com/statistics/227352/number-of-active-tencent-im-user-accounts-in-china/. Accessed 30 April 2020.
19. Hall C (2020) Weibo enters the e-commerce race. Should brands be excited or cautious? https://www.businessoffashion.com/articles/professional/weibo-enters-e-commerce-race-should-brands-be-excited-or-cautious. Accessed 4 May 2020.
20. GMA MarketingToChina (2020) Golden rules to social media marketing in China (updated 2020). https://www.marketingtochina.com/golden-rules-to-social-media-marketing-in-china-updated-2019/. Accessed 4 February 2021.
21. Jiang Y (2020) Secoo's 24-hour livestreams on Kuaishou are a big win. https://jingdaily.com/secoo-24-hour-livestreams-on-kuaishou-are-a-big-win/. Accessed 11 June 2020.
22. Hall C (2020) Weibo enters the e-commerce race. Should brands be excited or cautious? https://www.businessoffashion.com/articles/professional/weibo-enters-e-commerce-race-should-brands-be-excited-or-cautious. Accessed 4 May 2020.
23. Facebook (2020) Introducing Facebook shops: helping small businesses sell online. https://about.fb.com/news/2020/05/introducing-facebook-shops/. Accessed 19 May 2020.

4

Customer Centricity Is Key

Customers have never been so close to brands than today. This is the result of 20 years of evolution … from the first internet websites, collaborative internet (it was called 2.0), social network and platforms.
—Antonio Carriero, Chief Digital and Technology Officer of Breitling, Questionnaire Conducted by the Authors

Key Aspects

- Customer centricity is the growth elixir of luxury.
- Personalisation at scale calls for CRM and analytics.
- In particular, it is important to understand that the prospects are digital natives.
- HENRYs are a promising subgroup of millennials.
- Millennials are affluent customers, so luxury collaborations, authentic values and experiences are becoming more important to them.
- Chinese customers are driving more and more global trends in luxury.
- Chinese millennials are sophisticated customers with high expectations of personalised experiences.
- Local luxury shopping is on the rise.
- Digital natives reinforce business models like resale and rental.

In Chap. 1, we stated that new retail and omni-personal phygital are about customer centricity, and in Chap. 2, we defined luxury as an experience. Subsequently, we considered in Chap. 3 the previous approaches to combining luxury and the Internet, including the fundamental role of social media in creating omni-personal relationships. In this chapter, we focus on two core customer groups that are expected to drive the luxury growth in the upcoming years, Gen Y and Gen Z, as well as China. Both groups are experimenting with new consumption behaviours.

4.1 Experience Design Starts with Thinking Backwards from the Customer

The luxury strategy so far has been based on geographic expansion, which has led to the continuous opening of new stores, particularly in China. It is gradually becoming clear that this development is following the same pattern as in Japan on a much larger scale: the Chinese market is maturing faster than the industry expected, including the shift towards online. The fundamental challenge is to put the customers and their individual needs at the centre of the brand strategy, optimising their experiences and the business results. The ultimate brand relevance for an individual is achieved by addressing the individual in a personalised way. That personalisation at scale brings added value in terms of brand perception and revenue; simultaneously, it calls for CRM and analytics. This is something that appears to be less important in a world where 25 customers a day enter the flagship store of a French jewellery brand in Paris.[1] The necessary time and personalisation seem to be trackable with the help of a notebook. Of course, that changes dramatically in a world where the Watches & Wonders Livestream on Tmall Luxury Pavilion generates 800,000 views per streaming session.[2]

4.1.1 Millennials' Lifestyle and Consumption

We do not go online anymore—we live online. The future of luxury is digital because its future customers are digital natives: millennials, also known as Gen Y, born after 1981, and Gen Z, born after 1995. While Gen Y grew up and matured with the Internet and its possibilities, Gen Z cannot imagine a world without the Internet. The car, still a symbol of freedom for Gen X, has been replaced by the smartphone. Being mobile, connected, ethical, engaged, sustainable and well educated have become basic conditions for them—regardless of their gender or the culture to which they belong. The confrontation with war and disease takes place predominantly in the media, but the omni-present awareness of terror and misfortune gives them a strong desire for security and safety.

HENRYs

HENRYs (high earners not rich yet) form a particularly promising subgroup of millennials. Representing the next generation of luxury customers, they do not focus exclusively on material luxury goods as a status symbol or as self-rewards for being promoted. For them, the meaning is rooted in personal goals. Personal achievements matter more than financial success. This can refer to objectives such as running a marathon, writing a book, enjoying a self-determined life or making a trip around the world. In the end, everything is about self-expression. Who you are is more important than what you have.

Affluent Consumption

That mindset also explains why millennials are much more affluent customers than former generations. Mixing high and low is a widespread practice. If you do not force yourself into a life in the fast lane, you can easily mix high-fashion jewellery and a Gucci bag with jeans by H&M. This phenomenon occurs across categories and cultures. Another example is Chinese tourists who stay in low-budget hotels but afterwards invest heavily in luxury shopping. Fashion houses like Versace and Jimmy Choo play with that new consumption behaviour when they set up capsule collections with mass retailers like H&M. These campaigns attract affluent shoppers.

Targeting Millennials

We fell in love with the visionary words of a great man: 'They said prêt-à-porter will kill your name, and it saved me'—who else could have said these words other than unforgettable Pierre Cardin! And even if luxury is cautious, because there is a lot equity at stake—so there is disruption thanks to Pierre, but also when we think of smartwatches. Classical luxury timepieces have lost a good portion of their symbol status due to substitutes like smartphones and activity trackers, which signal a progressive, dynamic and healthy lifestyle. Luxury brand Hermès responded to that trend with the creation of a smartwatch in partnership with technology giant Apple. Perfectly matching glitter cases are available from Swarovski.[3] However, brands like Montblanc, Louis Vuitton and TAG Heuer have also developed smartwatches like the 'Montblanc Summit 2', 'Louis Vuitton Tambour Horizon' and 'TAG Heuer Carrera Connected'. After an initial attempt by TAG Heuer to target the upmarket luxury segment, it discovered HENRYs as its new core target group. Timepieces range between US$1000 and US$5000, and the high-performance claim

'Don't crack under pressure' targets top athletes and ambitious ladies. That is at least the implicit message when you look at brand testimonials from the likes of Super Bowl champion Tom Brady or supermodel Cara Delevingne. The connected smartwatch represents the icing on the cake as it is based on Google's Android operating system to compete with Hermès's Apple approach. As with any innovation, the new product, the new service, the new business model required risk analysis. The worst-case scenario is when the innovation does not generate a profit but costs a multi-million investment—in the case of Tag Heuer US$15 million. In short, nothing but expenses. Guy Sémon, Tag Heuer's Technical Director and Head of Product Development at the time, relied on the project's media attention.[4] When a classic watchmaker updates itself, it does not go unnoticed. In this respect, the millions can be chalked up as a marketing investment. If it crystallises that smartwatches are the future, then the journey has of course been worthwhile. The frontrunner stands in the front row, while it is too late for many competitors to play along.

That is also to the point of Kristian Tear, CEO of Bang & Olufsen, when outlining: 'Lastly we might also see more technology brands entering the luxury industry—or established brands launching new technology enabled products'. Bang & Olufsen is uniquely positioned to drive that evolvement forward. For the high-end consumer electronics brand digital is the core. In line with that, the brand has introduced a 'Product Health Center' allowing products to be connected to a cloud environment, enabling new self-service features for customers and remote management of the product from retail partners or customer service representatives. The 'Product Health Center' enables even the proactive detection of potential issues, remote diagnostics and deployment of fixes, before a customer would pay notice to the issue. 'Design products enabled by technology can give us insight into how, when, and where our customers engage with and use our products', concludes Kristian Tear, always considering that: 'Human interaction is likely to remain a premium currency for the coming years in luxury'.

In 2020, IWC launched a series of humorous sketches as part of its 'A smart watch. And a half' campaign. Within three YouTube clips, 85-year-old Kurt Klaus, who as a legendary watchmaker has translated the Gregorian calendar into a mechanical programme, plays a central role. In-store, the well-dressed gentleman is advised by a dynamic sales associate in a casual look on the smartwatch's advantages. They chat about watch settings, updates and durability—from the young salesman's point of view, everything is super easy and user-friendly. Simultaneously, his explanations lack simplicity in the ears of a mechanical watch connoisseur. A loving homage to the art of watchmaking that casts a smiling eye on smartwatches and mechanical watches. The moral of the story: It is in the beholder's eye to define what a 'smart' watch should be able to serve.

Besides the merge of technology and luxury, collaborations between watchmakers and fashion brands are entering the market, such as Jaeger-LeCoultre's Reverso by Christian Louboutin.[5] As an inspiring example of a partnership between a watchmaker and a football club, we want to highlight Hublot. The brand unveiled a smartwatch featuring an exclusive football app with the English Premier League. The 'Big Bang e Premier League' is an evolution of the initial smartwatch, now with the 'Hublot Loves Football Premier League' app pre-installed, which allows users to be alerted 15 minutes before the beginning of a Premier League match. It also displays goals, substitutions, penalties, added game time and other helpful information. The collection is limited to 200 pieces—not enough to satisfy all football enthusiasts but a new way to reach HENRYs through new experiences.

Call for Sustainability

Another strategy to engage with millennials is the focus on sustainability regarding environmental, ecological and social aspects. Apart from Rolex's omnipresence in social media and various exclusive sports events favoured by young people, the brand has initiated the 'Rolex Award for Enterprise' to honour start-ups and young entrepreneurs for exceptional sustainability and innovation projects, making our world a better place.[6] That better world is also targeted by brands like Chopard, Tiffany and De Beers. Raw materials, like gold, and precious stones, such as diamonds, are sometimes associated with war, bad working conditions, child labour and severe conflicts between people and countries. Despite the Kimberley Process and international conventions against child labour, the lack of supply chain transparency remains a bitter truth for many companies. Therefore, brands that take responsibility for sustainable and fair sourcing, trading and manufacturing processes stand out from the crowd.

Chopard has partnered with the Alliance for Responsible Mining (ARM), an NGO focusing on the well-being of gold miners. In 2013, the brand launched the first 'Green Carpet Collection' at the Cannes Film Festival, made purely out of fairly mined gold.[7] Tiffany started sourcing metals and diamonds from responsible mines only and introduced a zero-tolerance policy for diamonds from conflict regions. Last but not least, the diamond market leader De Beers launched Lightbox Jewelry, which uses lab-grown diamonds in its collections. Neither humans nor the environment is harmed, and lab-grown diamonds are 20 to 30 per cent cheaper than traditionally mined stones. For millennials, that is a striking deal linked to a story that is proudly spread without shame.

The Value of Self-Expression
Gaining part of the brand story and not just consuming matters to millennials. Only by having a unique personal experience online or in store and sharing it as a kind of self-expression via social networks does the relationship with a brand become meaningful to them. In accordance with the motto 'live and travel, a selfie provides proof'. Therefore, the mobile phone is a survival tool to nurture a person's digital image. The ego is taking selfies, sharing consumption experiences and connecting the real seamlessly with the virtual. For digital natives, it is absolutely normal to live in this way. Millennials enjoy content, emotions and relationships. They love self-expression and authentic responsibility because actions speak louder than words. The opposite of self-expression is not listening to others. It is ignorance. We should be aware of that in brand communication as the title 'luxury brand' is earned based on actions and effects.

4.1.2 China: Other Cultures, Other Habits

In addition to the growth potential of millennials, a special focus of luxury is on Chinese customers, not only because Swiss watch exports to mainland China rose while everywhere else watch exports decreased heavily but also because China is increasingly setting new global trends. COVID-19 is achieving more than just continuing that transformation: it is accelerating the industry disruption, and the 'copy to China' approach is turning into the 'copy from China' approach. Social commerce and live streaming, as discussed in Sect 3.2.2 in Chap. 3, are just one example, but fashion and styling trends are also being born in China, like the latest hype around young men wearing pearl earrings.[8] In other words, pearl jewellery is expanding its reach in China today and maybe in the rest of the world tomorrow. Beyond, brands with Chinese origin, like Blanc de Chine, have opened Western stores in New York, Paris and other cities.

Status, Success, Wealth
As in many other Asian countries, in China, collectivism is traditionally important, but the one-child policy dating back to 1979 has created a new generation of princesses and princes. Pampered by their parents and

grandparents, they are driven by the high expectations of their parents and self-reward themselves with luxury consumption. However, luxury consumption in China extends beyond the ego: a person needs to look good to make the whole family look good. That matter of reputation is called 'Mien-tzu' and is similar to Veblen's conspicuous consumption concept. Luxury consumption in China expresses social status, success and wealth.[9] The Chinese only child is much more individualistic and confident in terms of style and taste, as this generation is used to being at the centre of attention. That makes Chinese millennials sophisticated customers.

Data-Driven Personalisation
On the one hand, customers' expectations of personalised experiences are very high as the luxury market matures. Realising that possessing items is not the only path to happiness makes people curious about experiential luxury. On the other hand, Chinese customers share large amounts of personal data without any concerns, and these data simplify the personal experience design, even if it still needs to be structured smartly.

Data capturing comes with complexity. According to a study conducted in 2019, in the product research phase, Chinese customers tended to interact with a brand across 4 to 5 and up to 15 touchpoints, and 60 per cent of those interactions were digital. Still, the in-store purchase action remained 88 per cent.[10] Since the research phase is such an important one in China, online product descriptions should be extremely detailed to answer potential questions and to build trust.

Going Glocal
In parallel, touchpoints are expanding from international metropolises towards local luxury shopping, including Chinese second-tier and third-tier cities. Daigou, the practice of Chinese people shopping for luxury goods at better rates abroad and bringing them back home, is becoming less attractive due to the global price harmonisation of luxury brands, as introduced by brands like Chanel. On top, the COVID-19 crisis is showing us today a world with extremely weak travel retail. Furthermore, the Chinese government has increased duties, and agents for overseas purchases have experienced further regulation. In response, local shopping and resale businesses are on the rise. Watchmaker Vacheron Constantin kicked off targeted WeChat advertising in second-tier cities like Tianjin and Shijiazhuang, as it means developing consumption locally and not through trans-shipping.

In conclusion, an expansion strategy towards local shopping will be the key as we can already observe today that about half of Tmall's Luxury Pavilion sales are routed back to customers living outside first-tier and second-tier cities in China. Chinese millennials are just accelerating that transformation. To ensure that Western brands keep their position in the relevant set of Chinese customers, companies like YNAP and Farfetch have teamed up with Chinese players Alibaba and JD.

Deep Dive: YNAP, Alibaba, Farfetch and JD in China

- The low level of infrastructure and logistics maturity in smaller Chinese cities has made it extremely difficult for Western brands to ensure a luxurious delivery experience in the past. That is one of the reasons why local expertise is so beneficial. The other reason is the immense traffic that Tmall and JD consolidate on their platform. Therefore, YNAP teamed up with Alibaba and launched its Net-a-Porter flagship store in Tmall Luxury Pavilion, while JD merged its high-end platform Top Life with Farfetch China in 2017.
- Farfetch received the required customer data and logistics in exchange for sharing its technology and direct platform access to its luxury marketplace with JD's Top Life. In the meantime, Top Life has been fully integrated into Farfetch. In general, JD's audience is spreading across the country, with a special focus on North China, Sichuan and lower-tier cities. In terms of shipping, orders are dispatched from JD's warehouse or directly from the brand through the e-commerce shop operator. To complete the package, an exclusive white-glove service is available to deliver luxury goods in style.
- In 2018, YNAP launched its joint venture Feng Mao in collaboration with Alibaba besides the Tmall Luxury Pavilion store. In contrast to JD, Tmall is clearly more focused on the Yangtze Delta, Guang Dong and the Central Plain. The packaging is processed and shipped by the brands, and an external third-party delivery service, SF Express, is available.
- Both YNAP and Farfetch offer concepts to support the entry for Western brands into the Chinese market through their partnership models with Chinese ecosystems from content production and social media to payment and CRM tools. An important goal of those services is to shift the sales ambassador focus from administration to service and the customer focus from product availability to experience. That new retail approach has even convinced highly protective brands like Chanel to set up a partnership with Farfetch to make different scenarios possible, such as identifying customers via an installed mobile application at the moment of entering the 'store of the future'.

4.2 Customers Experiment with New Consumption Behaviours

Not only are millennials and Chinese customers setting luxury industry trends but also their consumption behaviour is calling for new business models, namely resale and rental. The two models have in common that the possession of material luxury is seen as a temporary experience and not as ownership for the purpose of ownership. The motivation of both behaviours is rooted in the relentless search for the new, access to variety, the wish to declutter and, last but not least, sustainability. The collecting mania of our grandparents, caused by times of need, is now increasingly frowned upon and has been replaced by the throw-away society with an awakening aspiration for more awareness. Millennials are looking for socially and environmentally compatible ways to enjoy the extraordinary. While resale stands for the replacement of possession, rental refers to the pure pleasure of the consumption moment.

Rental Model

At this stage, companies like Rent the Runway are leading the rental business by making extraordinary designer fashion pieces available, if and when they are needed, for an affordable subscription fee of less than US$200 per month. Based on the subscription model, customers are becoming used to the service. Millennials especially are demanding rental models in luxury. Today most luxury rental models are specialised companies, but in the future luxury brands and conglomerates will take over more ownership of the business to maintain full control over the presentation and communication of their iconic pieces. Moreover, the subscription model is a convincing way to reinforce customer loyalty. On the one hand, it constitutes an extension of the rental business, but, on the other hand, it is a business model in its own right.

Purchasing in Instalments

The start-up Watchdreamer offers luxury watch purchases in instalments. The company provides the opportunity to buy a luxury watch through a loan that is repaid over a period of 12 to 48 months. Not all watchmakers are in favour of this practice, but it definitely helps to make exclusive timepieces affordable to new customer segments. Nevertheless, it is a business model with the potential to become an integral part of future luxury e-commerce platforms.

Resale Model
That brings us to the resale model. The conglomerate Kering invested in the second-hand platform Vestiaire Collective, and Richemont acquired the second-hand platform Watchfinder to take the pole position in luxury timepiece resale. That is fully in line with the wish of 73 per cent of customers to sell their used luxury goods back to the brands instead of hoarding items or giving them to friends and family members.

Making Luxury Affordable
It is noteworthy that resale, rental, consignment and subscription models are based on new consumption behaviours while strategically cultivating that new behaviour in the sense of making luxury an affordable lifestyle. Besides that, we can notice a lasting effect on the customer journey of millennials, meaning that many customers search for resale platforms first to understand the willingness to pay for a certain item. That tells them about the potential of their own investment when they make a buying decision one day and decide to resell another day.

The past of luxury was not a customer-led one. Today, customers are in the driving seat, and companies need to listen to them: integrating their personal preferences will be the future. The disruption is bigger than you would think since the boundaries between industries, products, services and channels are blurring, breaking all the previous codes. Luxury companies will need to be more agile and adapt to avoid the risk of missing the new generations. Customer centricity is not achieved by understanding customers across your touchpoints and your journey; it is about their touchpoints with your brand.

In summary, internal brand data will not be enough to understand your customers fully. Strategic alliances and consortiums with the objective of sharing data and client knowledge will arise in the future. These will allow deeper insights and a truly holistic view (e.g., Alibaba Brand Databank). However, that additional knowledge needs to remain balanced with the clients' preferences. The omni-personal approach respects the client and builds on shared data, not on forced data. That is an essential aspect to prevent becoming invasive to the customer. Whenever you are in doubt of the right barriers, put yourself in the shoes of your customer and remind you to Brunello Cucinelli's words to act as 'butlers, not stalkers'.

Notes

1. Chevalier M, Gutsatz M (eds) (2019) Luxury retail and digital management. Wiley, New Jersey, Location 3982.
2. Canaves S (2020) Hard luxury gets the livestreaming treatment. https://jingdaily.com/hard-luxury-gets-the-livestreaming-treatment. Accessed 30 April 2020.
3. Swarovski (2020) Company website. https://www.swarovski.com/en-DE/c-0311/Categories/Accessories/Cases-compatible-with-Apple-Watch-/. Accessed 2 August 2020.
4. Monteiro, F., The TAG Heuer Carrera Connected Watch (A): Swiss Avant-Garde for the Digital Age, pp. 11–14.
5. Doerr E (2016) Jaeger-LeCoultre joins forces with shoe designer Christian Louboutin on Atelier Reverso line. https://www.forbes.com/sites/elizabethdoerr/2016/01/26/jaeger-lecoultre-joins-forces-with-shoe-designer-christian-louboutin-on-atelier-reverso-line/#607bcfa7fdc2. Accessed 26 January 2021.
6. Rolex (2020) Company website. https://www.rolex.org/en/rolex-awards. Accessed 2 August 2020.
7. Chopard (2020) Company website. https://www.chopard.com/intl/green-carpet-collection. Accessed 2 August 2020.
8. Luo J (2020) The importance of China's Gen Z men in pearl earrings. https://jingdaily.com/the-importance-of-chinas-gen-z-men-in-pearl-earrings/. Accessed 26 July 2020.
9. Chadha R, Husband P (2006) The cult of the luxury brand: Inside Asia's love affair with luxury. Nicholas Brealey International, London, p 129.
10. Chang A, Mauron P (2020) JingDigital and Digital Luxury Group—WeChat luxury index 2020. JingDigital. https://www.jingdigital.com/en/articles/8255/, p 7. Accessed 3 April 2021.

5

Digital Transformation of the Omni-personal Customer Journey

It is the how I am going to adapt to what the client needs. You cannot standardize this. When the client enters the store, give him a cup of coffee, a glass of water or champagne, but in the end this is not where you make the difference. You make a difference on showing your real love. And showing your real love is not only about selling a watch but listening to the customer and read between lines. That is the biggest change in 2020. At AP we call it people-to-people.
—François-Henry Bennahmias CEO at Audemars Piguet, Questionnaire Conducted by the Authors

Key Aspects

- The omni-personal experience builds on Memory, Empathy, Real time and Consistency (the MERC factors) across channels and touchpoints.
- Those MERC factors need to be omnipresent across the phases of the customer journey cycle.
- In the awareness phase, the customer consent is the maximum brand commitment as it opens the possibility of further one-to-one engagement.
- In the engagement phase, a brand needs to convince and eliminate individual customer doubts to lead seamlessly into conversion.
- The conversion phase should be dominated by perfection, excitement and satisfaction.
- Fulfilment is not about basics but about enthusiasm factors, surprising the customer positively and innovatively.
- The after-sales phase should guarantee personalised services to enhance the brand loyalty.

- Analytics support the iterative process to deepen one-to-one relationships in an omni-personal customer journey.

Do not forget the customer; that person could be you. Nevertheless, many companies show advanced amnesia when we buy an article online and visit the store one day later. You think you talked to them recently and want to be remembered, but actually your sales associate does not recognise you at all. Unless you are one of his or her personal VIP customers, the sales associate cannot remember your last purchase, your last request or your last touchpoint, not to mention your last name. Imagine the pleasure gained from a welcoming atmosphere in which you meet a person who knows who you are, whom you have met in the past and who maybe even knows your needs. We all have enough fantasy to know what makes us feel better, and feeling better probably translates into buying again or at least developing a meaningful relationship. At Audemars Piguet, CEO François-Henry Bennahmias refers to it as 'bringing back the human connections'.

Customer Journey Models

Attention, interest and desire, in their linear beauty, do not necessarily explain actions. This statement is still true, but it does not capture the complexity of human behaviour and belief. McKinsey's customer decision journey (CDJ) from 2009 replaced the AIDA funnel based on attention, interest, desire and action through a circular model looping consideration, evaluation and research, purchase and post-purchase experience, resulting in loyalty (Figs. 5.1 and 5.2). It is still applicable but no longer reflects the most important protagonist of every sales experience: the customer as an individual.

The world has become an experience, and we are mature enough to talk openly about emotions. Life has become a journey, and selling is one of the possible actions within this journey. When we aim to increase the probability of that event, we need strong relationships. We need to act omni-personally and meaningfully: not in the perception of the abstract customer John Doe, Jean Dupont or Max Mustermann but in the individual eyes of a unique person with unique needs, expectations and emotions. That person could be you. That is why we developed the omni-personal model to support brands in their transformation from omni-channel to omni-personal experiences:

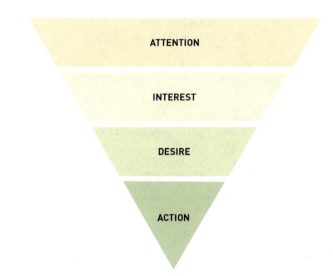

Fig. 5.1 The AIDA funnel model (Lewis, 1898)

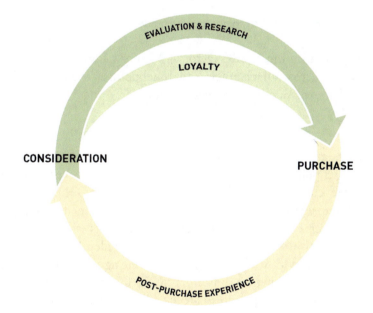

Fig. 5.2 The CDJ customer decision journey model (McKinsey, 2009)

The Omni-personal Customer Journey Model

The omni-personal model puts the individual customer at the centre to enable brands to create omni-personal experiences at scale with the ultimate objective of gaining the loyalty of individuals (Fig. 5.3). The omni-personal

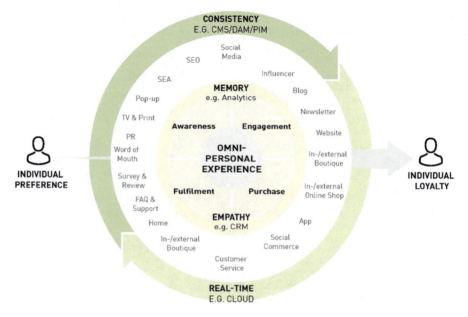

Fig. 5.3 The Omni-personal customer journey model

experience builds on the MERC factors – Memory, Empathy, Real time and Consistency – across all channels and touchpoints. These MERC factors require further explanation, as provided below.

Memory

As long as an individual is consistently connecting with a brand via one exclusive touchpoint, it is easy to understand and maybe even to remember, which is the current phase of the customer journey. The omni-channel approach increases the amount of data and the complexity and in proportion the ability to remember a specific customer. Analytics is our best friend in tracking customer interactions at scale. It is used to identify where and how a customer interacts with which product. After setting up all the requirements and relevant key performance indicators (KPIs) for analytics, the major challenge is to translate big data into smart data, besides aggregating internal and external data sources. In conclusion, analytics is our memory tool. It allows us to *listen* to the customer.

Empathy

The best-quality data have no value when we do not use them to derive individual preferences. To personalise all communication, we need to exploit the full potential of CRM to obtain a 360-degree view of our customers, potentially with the support of a customer data platform (CDP). Furthermore, we need to show that we can translate our data knowledge into empathy. It is amazing to know someone's birthday, but this knowledge is completely useless if we send a super generic happy birthday e-mail that ends up in the spam folder of the lucky recipient. As Jean-Jacques Rousseau stated, '*Smell* is the sense of memory and desire'. The two together blend into empathy, and the CRM ecosystem is the fundamental tool to allow empathy at scale.

Real Time

At the moment when a customer enters a store, the communication needs to be relevant. To act appropriately based on the given context, upfront data and recommendations help the sales associate to increase the relevance. In other words, before a customer enters the store, the sales associate needs access to personal data like his or her name and even the sales history, if available. That is where real-time data make the big difference, as it is vital to obtain the data on time. Once the customer has left the store, it is too late to become aware of potential up- and cross-selling opportunities. Figuratively, it would be like receiving birthday congratulations one week late. The pleasure is not the same. It does not have the same effect. The right word at the right time counts, and it means that we need to *communicate* with the customer fluently, in the customer's preferred language and in real time. In an omni-channel world, cloud services allow us to do so as they enable real-time data synchronisation across channels and touchpoints.

Consistency

Here we are repeating ourselves. In a small world, it is easy to be consistent, but in a big world, ensuring that all the channels and touchpoints show what we intend customers to *see* is a complex task. The CMS, DAM and PIM platforms address that need, as they act as consistent sources of truth for content elements such as images, videos and other digital formats, which enable an ecosystem approach to distribute content to multiple applications, such as product catalogues or advertising tools. Consistent brand and product presentation foster trust.

All four factors are essential for relevant, personal, fluent and consistent dialogue and for relationship building at eye level between a brand and an individual. Hence, the MERC factors need to be omnipresent throughout all the phases of the customer journey cycle (the inner circle)—awareness, engagement, purchase and fulfilment, including after-sales activity—to establish and reinforce the loyalty of the individual with each direct or indirect interaction with a brand touchpoint (outer circle).

Loyalty
Loyalty is the result of a self-reinforcing cycle that deepens the relationship to the ultimate status of brand love. It makes the difference between habitual buyer and persuasion buyer. Both are loyal and link emotions to the brand: security and simplification versus passion and love. However, a person who is in love with a brand has much more influence as a brand ambassador than one who consumes mainly for rational reasons. The more omni-personalisation that an individual experiences during the customer journey, the greater is his or her tendency to be *touched* by a brand and to fall in love and therefore the higher is the emotional bonding, loyalty and revenue potential associated with that individual. The fact that loyalty drives profits and growth has been proven,[1] but we aim to prove the link between omni-personalisation at scale and loyalty.

We have talked about the golden side of the coin to reinforce loyalty. Nevertheless, we should not forget that loyalty is easily lost if brands constantly ignore the individual preferences of a person. Imagine that you have already bought an exclusive timepiece at brand X and mentioned several times in store as well as in the online filter settings that you do not like yellow gold at all. Still, you receive one recommendation after another for timepieces in yellow gold. All the hard-earned loyalty is at risk when you face the fair perception that no one is really listening to you—to the point at which you become open to conversations with brand Y, given that brand Y takes care of your personal preferences more consciously.

Differentiation Between the AIDA Model and the CDJ Model
The dynamic impact of personal experience on a person's loyalty does not necessarily mean that the engagement or evaluation and research phase will be skipped or accelerated, as indicated by McKinsey's CDJ model. In the luxury segment, the product engagement phase remains a critical part of the customer experience even for loyal customers. For example, the fact that you already own a Pomellato Nudo ring with blue topaz does not mean that you will skip the product try-on experience when you are buying another Nudo ring with white topaz. You would like to enjoy the full experience.

In conclusion, the CDJ model does not consider luxury specifics, while the AIDA model is not made with synchronous interaction across multiple touchpoints in mind. That means that the omni-channel cannot be reflected in the AIDA logic. It is also the reason why we do not link touchpoints explicitly to the quadrants of the customer journey phases. Social media, for example, are relevant throughout all the phases of the customer journey.

The following subchapters are structured according to the key customer journey phases to provide an overview of the innovation potential, use cases and deep dives, spiced with insights gained through questionnaires completed by luxury industry leaders.

5.1 Generate Awareness to Be Considered as Part of the Relevant Set

The thing is, I do not want to be sold to when I walk into a store. I want to be welcomed.
 —Angela Ahrendts, Former CEO at Burberry and Senior Vice President at Apple Retail

You see the timepiece of your dreams on the wrist of a good friend, and he tells you proudly that it is an Omega Speedmaster. You find the Love bracelet in a new variation posted on Instagram and give it an intuitive like. When flipping through a magazine, your eyes are caught by the Bulgari Octo. You google 'iconic diamond ring' and see Harry Winston advertising. You search for 'lightest automatic watch' and explore blog articles about Richard Mille's 32-gram RM 67-02. Imagine that you are a man and have never thought about shopping at Tiffany for yourself when you enter the pop-up store at 6 East 57th Street in New York. In 2019, the brand launched its first official men's collection, including high jewellery pieces like rings and earrings for men, besides games and iconic sports trophies.[2] Your girlfriend is window shopping and gives you a clear hint that her next Christmas gift should come in a Pomellato shopping bag and that, of course, the content matters.

In these and many similar situations, it makes no difference whether you are actively searching for something or whether you are inspired by beauty or even by the desire of your loved ones. The initial moment of truth in the customer journey is the moment when you are confronted with a brand for the first time because you are looking for entertainment or something in particular. As we have seen, the touchpoints may be incredibly diverse. All those magic moments have in common that you connect with and are welcomed into the brand universe: it might happen online, offline or in a directly operated or franchised store. It is like looking for the first time into the eyes of a potential partner: either it awakens the curiosity for more or it does not.

Ultimately a brand becomes part of the relevant set considered by the customer, and indeed, the awareness of a brand is not the end of the game. The awareness of a brand will continue with the awareness of a certain collection, the awareness of a certain piece of art and the awareness of something unique and personal that is not replicable at all. That is also why luxury never refers to products as products: it is about precious creations and pieces of art, iconic timepieces and timekeepers. In that first phase, an individual's opting in is the maximum commitment that you can obtain as it opens the door for further engagement with the brand.

5.1.1 In-Store Augmented and Virtual Reality Applications Bring the Brand Universe to Life

The first transformation is about 'integrated retail', not only e-commerce becoming an important channel but also digital and physical being totally interwoven.

The second transformation is that retail is media, and media is retail.

—Cyrille Vigneron, CEO at Cartier, Questionnaire Conducted by the Authors

First and foremost, the in-store experience remains the key for luxury as it is the guarantee of immersive experiences. The store is the place where Monsieur Cartier and Coco Chanel found a playground to keep full control over the game between artist and admirer, between entrepreneur and customer. The CRM system at that time was still a mental hard disc nurtured by pen and paper, but it was already a central element for building empathic relationships. Today, the distribution channels are too complex to remember each customer by heart, but the need for customised multi-sensorial experiences remains. Mystery shopping visits and checklists are great tools to ensure harmonised service and brand presentation. CRM platforms demand and encourage our memory, but more is necessary: we need to translate all information into actionable insights to create personalised experiences.

The first in-store visit of a prospective client is a perfect chance to understand those individual needs and preferences better. In-store cameras and sensors capture movement and interaction profiles. The sales associate collects personal preferences. Last but not least, augmented and virtual reality tools decode motivation patterns. The game changer is called phygital experience design and aims to activate mutual empathy. That requires humans and technology to merge forces to understand the customer, even if the customer's action is not congruent with what he or she has told you verbally.

5 Digital Transformation of the Omni-personal Customer Journey

As a simple example, a lady enters the store and tells you that she would just like to have a look to be inspired, but after a short seeking glance, she immediately moves in the direction of a certain piece. In other words, her targeted action signals to you that she is probably already aware of her desire, has browsed the website upfront and is now looking for a try-on experience. As another example, a man enters the store and asks the sales associate if the timepiece model displayed in the window is available with a stainless steel strap. The sales associate reports that is not available right now in the store but invites the man to enjoy the stainless steel version as part of a virtual reality session on an interactive digital screen. Surprisingly, within that virtual session, the man pays special attention to rubber straps. He probably prefers a modern sporty look or is simply looking for materials that are insensitive to temperature. That question should trigger a conversation and a data entry in the CRM system.

Empathy, excitement and entertainment drive all welcome ceremonies, and the sales associate acts as the master of ceremonies. Luxury stores typically have closed doors with a bell and a security guard. The windows are product displays that do not reveal what is hidden behind them in the showroom. A jeweller or watchmaker is like a mysterious treasure chest from the outside, seducing but not explicitly inviting. Inside, the visitor awaits a museum-style presentation—the products are displayed generously and inaccessibly in glass showcases.

That installation is part of the overall artwork, and it is up to the sales associate to break the ice and give the prospective customer the feeling of belonging and appreciation by offering beverages, making good conversation and opening the showcases. Munich-based jeweller Renèsim defined a living room atmosphere as its goal to make visitors feel as if they are at home and not in a temple.[3] Especially for younger generations, that atmosphere is essential. Regardless of their age, though, all customers agree that they expect to experience something unique. That uniqueness is increasingly based on augmented or virtual reality innovation.

Virtual Reality
We have five senses, but using them in new perspectives opens new worlds. Wearing Oculus Rift glasses is one example, as demonstrated by the watchmaker Oris. Counting on the fact that young target groups are excited by virtual reality (VR) applications and trusting that 80 per cent of them will happily share their first VR touchpoint with their friends,[4] the brand has built an application to see inside a watch in collaboration with Mackevision (Fig. 5.4).[5] The VR application supported the launch of the skeleton watch

Fig. 5.4 Computer-generated image, Oris SA, Watch Inside a Watch, 2019 (Printed with Oris SA permission)

'Big Crown ProPilot X Calibre 115 Sample 2' at Baselworld and provided a realistic view of the functioning of the mechanical movement. Accompanied by the constant ticking sound, the user could explore the aesthetics of light and perspective, spring and gear as well as the magic of time. The immersive experience was built based on a digital twin of the timepiece, allowing all the visuals to be integrated into an omni-channel communication strategy. The brand displayed 360-degree videos in store to attract younger generations and used visuals for PR and the online shop.

Deep Dive: Digital Twins, Computer-Generated Imagery (CGI) and Autonomous Sensory Meridian Response (ASMR)

The fascination with computer-generated images and digital twins is due to the impression of being able to see more. The level of detail, without sacrificing the depth of reality, is enormous. The high-resolution images are made to be touched and animated to activate new perspectives and emotions in the viewer's mind. That is why computer-generated images are a great tool for luxury brands to enhance the visual effect. Materials appear photo-realistic, and colours can easily be adjusted with a few mouse clicks. Bang & Olufsen is among the brands who identified the digitalisation of the content production as key. Kristian Tear, CEO of the Danish high-end consumer electronics company, shared with us:

5 Digital Transformation of the Omni-personal Customer Journey

We have leveraged CGI to produce 3D models of home settings, material types (wood structures, metal finishing etc.) and product variants to generate thousands of product and lifestyle assets without the need to touch a traditional studio. This has helped us realise significant cost savings, faster delivery times and increase of output, and more importantly it has enabled us to continue our marketing campaigning activities throughout times of travel bans and lockdowns where traditional campaign shoots were not an option.

Digital twins are not yet commonly used, but with the example of Bang & Olufsen we can see how usefully they can support companies throughout the value chain. Once a digital twin has been created—potentially even just the visualisation of a prototype that does not yet exist in reality—it assists internal processes like design and manufacturing as well as all brand communication and marketing activities. Therefore, experts like Mackevision, the Fabricant, Point Flottant, Cyreal and Threedium refer to the cost and time efficiency advantages of CGI following the 'single-source production' principle. This allows companies to produce high-quality content at scale, manageable via classical CMS tools. CGI enables us to see more than we would normally see thanks to the high resolution. Consequently, CGI translates into an extension of our five senses.

Autonomous sensory meridian response (ASMR) complements CGI. It relates to concepts of auditory–tactile synaesthesia and frisson and describes tingling sensations starting from the head triggered by multi-sensorial experiences. ASMR allows us to move beyond the photo-realistic reality by adding extra layers of perception. In a digital format, the applied sounds and images are cross-linked to further senses to enrich the effect. You listen to the whispering voice while having the feeling of being touched. You see diamonds on a timepiece that sit like sweet sugar crystals on the rim of a martini glass. You enjoy watching the liquid transformation of floral jewellery ornaments into a delicately fragrant bouquet of flowers. That is what ASMR can do for us: it builds conscious and unconscious analogies for our senses. That is a natural match to the multi-sensorial world of luxury.

To sum up, CGI can integrate the principles of ASMR to strengthen the multi-sensorial perception in product presentation and advertising across touchpoints and channels. The resulting content is no longer just the photo-realistic digital twin of a product but a unique emotional experience that integrates surreal elements of creativity and brand actualisation. We can understand it as a kind of digital brand meditation, and meditation here is meant not in the sense of relaxation but in the sense of deepening.

Another impressive example of virtual reality in store and beyond is Gucci's spring–summer campaign 2018, created by the Spanish artist Ignasi Monreal.[6] The artist introduced the Gucci gallery within the 'Gucci Hallucination' video. He demonstrated its immersive character by becoming part of one of his artworks, transforming into virtual reality at the moment of touching the painting. The blending of art and virtual reality is the main idea behind the campaign and is expressed at various touchpoints: the Gucci application allows customers to scan ads in store or in magazines to enter Monreal's animated paintings virtually. That use case is particularly interesting as it illustrates the seamless phygital approach. In-store windows and even the sales receipt show scannable stickers and artwork to engage customers to explore more.

Augmented Reality and Holograms
Augmented reality (AR) describes the enriching play of blending virtual elements into the real world. It can be a smart mirror allowing visitors to travel in time and a product gallery. It might be an augmented product try-on (see Sect. 5.2.2) via mobile phone or even the display of how-to guidelines in holographic headsets. It offers additional information to enrich reality with data, visuals and fiction.

Augmented reality can even lead to the point at which we gain ownership of digital twins, also known as non-fungible tokens (NFTs). Gucci partnered with the AR platform Wanna to create virtual sneakers.[7] In April 2021, the first digital watch twin of an NFT, encrypted via the blockchain Ethereum, was sold during an action, while the physical version of the 'Bigger Bang All Black Tourbillon Chronograph' remained in the ownership of Hublot's former Chairman, Jean-Claude Biver.[8] In that example, digital progressed beyond product visualisation and became luxury itself. This refers to crypto luxury collectibles and needs to be seen in the context of digital identity and blockchain (see Sect. 5.4.1).

Returning to the primary purpose of augmented reality to enrich reality, holograms are a sub-category of augmented reality. They are a pure version of augmented reality with higher rendering quality. Brands like Cartier are known for their hologram initiatives. In 1972, the brand captured significant attention for its 360-degree window projection of a lady's wrist with a diamond bracelet on New York's Fifth Avenue.[9] Several hologram initiatives followed and have updated the brand image over the last years as the technology allows extraordinary presentation and directs attention and customers to the inside of the store. Recently, Cartier presented a jewellery hologram installation at China's International Import Expo.[10] Visitors control the rotation and zoom in to capture all the details of 33 different creations. The corresponding sketch images are displayed next to the hologram on an interactive screen, entitled 'Do You Speak Cartier?'

Differentiating Virtual and Augmented Reality
All the preceding examples describe the fluent transition from attention to engagement and indicate that the individual customer journey accelerates through the application of virtual and augmented reality. While virtual reality takes the user into a fully computer-generated environment, augmented reality blends virtual elements with the real environment. We find it in digital try-on applications. VR applications in general have higher technical requirements than AR due to the graphics card, processor power and RAM needed to run VR applications. AR and VR offer a perfect chance to extend the time spent in store and bridge waiting times in store. There is no need to highlight that, for customers, interaction feels much better than just waiting. In the case that a family needs to wait while daddy enjoys a try-on session, or the required expert is still interacting with another customer, or in the case that the prospect is looking for inspiration, this could be the perfect time for the sales associate to invite the visitor to engage in a new experience. Waiting time or not, it is highly recommended to guide customers through the experience, preventing potential frustration due to technical complexity or motion sickness. The latter decreases with high-quality design and image resolution but still occurs as individually as seasickness.

We have also seen that different technologies can be applied in the AR and VR context: headsets, mobile devices, such as smartphones, and projection displays for holograms. Different mobility levels and costs are linked to those technologies. Of course, the software, experience design and 3D content creation are also not free. Therefore, it is important to derive a strategy building on synergies and scalability.

How to Build Virtual Experiences
Before you build a virtual experience, you should always define a strategy and ask yourself about the added value for the customer. That is your objective. The best case is to find an emotional answer like hedonism or self-esteem as well as a cognitive one linked to measurable values like convenience and time or cost efficiency.[11] You can define the use case and storytelling of an experience in line with the brand myth. You should certainly also test and validate

all the assumptions made so far before selecting the right digital tool and building the virtual experience. Of course, the moment of truth is when you look at the KPIs and prove the concept. In the case of success, you make the experience available to customers and kick off the marketing machine. In an ideal experience, the customers become part of that experience-at-scale process through their social media involvement.

In conclusion, augmented reality and virtual reality are helpful tools to reinvent in-store experiences, which are no longer product-driven presentations but personalised, sensorial and emotional experiences. These experiences express all the creativity and uniqueness of a brand and its customers and clearly differentiate it from the competitor next door. However, if poorly executed, augmented and virtual reality are not more than gadgets. Fundamentally, the objective should be to move beyond making a virtual copy of the real world to create a parallel or extended world. That is where you can create unique stories, coordinated through the different virtual experience layers and thus complementing reality. Similar to the example of the Gucci use case, you can imagine a virtual timepiece exhibition. Via magazines, out-of-home advertising, digital windows or in-store campaigns, you can invite people into your virtual store by delivering experience nuggets—emotionally strong enough to be shareable on social media. Ultimately, you can envisage a phygital room in your store to enable a physical visit to the virtual timepiece exhibition. That is of particular interest in relation to historical timepieces, which are not available in the standard assortment of the store.

5.1.2 When Pop-Up Stores and Partnering with Museums Build Brand Knowledge

The boundary between store and museum is often fluid, like the boundary between luxury and art. Pop-up stores and collaborations with museums create a natural extension of the in-store brand presentation, satisfying the main purpose of entertaining and educating about the brand and its iconic items. Its objective is to make the individual prospect and customer a brand expert or at least a community insider, understanding the history and uniqueness of products. Naturally, we are referring here not only to brand awareness but also to loyalty.

Differing from their modern interpretation, the first pop-up stores organised by luxury brands like Cartier were purely offline events: linked to seasonal highlights like Christmas or Valentine's Day, hundreds of personal invitation letters were handwritten and sent out to the target audience to

5 Digital Transformation of the Omni-personal Customer Journey

attract attention to new collection launches. Today, pop-up events intrigue with innovation and engaging experiences (Fig. 5.5). In the introduction to this chapter, we mentioned Tiffany's pop-up store for men. Further examples are Marc Jacobs's pop-up store in 2014, which accepted social media posts with the hashtag #MJDaisyChain as a virtual currency to pay for products,[12] and two years later, Louis Vuitton's fully personalised pop-up store in brand colours, completely printed in 3D technology within only two weeks.[13] In 2020, Louis Vuitton launched a mobile store in a caravan to overcome the COVID-19 barriers with a maximum personalisation service.[14] If the prophet does not come to the mountain, the mountain must come to the prophet.

Today, we all know that online pop-ups have become common practice with the increased usage of mobile phones. A good example is Tiffany's pop-up Tmall Luxury Pavilion, designed to launch its new Tiffany Paper Flowers collection in 2018.[15] Since that, many other brands followed with differentiated initiatives and campaigns, leveraging platforms like Tmall.

The benefits of a pop-up range from introducing new collections and reaching new target groups to brand education and testing new store concepts in an industry that otherwise does not allow testing with customer involvement. Pop-ups open up the playground for new experiences and new target groups

Fig. 5.5 Pop-up events intrigue with innovation and engaging experiences (Image: Fxquadro—stock.adobe.com)

that would resist traditional store formats. They are an invitation to interact with a brand. Furthermore, in a B2B context, pop-ups offer an effective public relations tool to connect with relevant opinion leaders and journalists while setting an exclusive scene for product launches due to the temporary character of the stage.

Beyond the presentation of the latest collection in spacious in-store galleries, dedicated exhibitions in collaboration with leading art museums are a common strategy in the luxury segment. We are referring to luxury brands that run their own art foundations, such as the 'Fondation Louis Vuitton pour la Création', 'Foundation F Pinault for Modern and Contemporary Art', 'Cartier Foundation for Contemporary Art' and 'Prada Fondazione', as well as watchmakers, for instance the 'Patek Philippe Museum'. Luxury builds timelessness based on its past and history. In museums, everyone feels comfortable as nothing more is expected than watching and appreciating art in a great environment. Chaumet and Boucheron demonstrate that private museums, as part of their flagship stores at Place Vendôme, can open the hearts and wallets of prestigious customers.

While online pop-up stores are nothing new, virtual museum visits are attracting more and more interest as a logical consequence of the COVID-19 restrictions. Hence, the Louvre and Centre Pompidou in Paris, the British Museum in London or the Museum of Fine Arts Boston have worked on new ways to bring art into living rooms. You can visit the British Museum on Google Street View and discover virtually more than 60 galleries besides the galleries on the website, a museum podcast and audio tours on Apple and YouTube Music.[16] On the International Museum Day, the Museum of Fine Arts Boston partnered with the Chinese live-streaming platform Kuaishou to host a four-hour live-streaming in which it offered viewers a range of Monet-related cultural products.[17] That initiative differed from similar initiatives by international museums, as it was almost entirely commercial. While previous museum live-streams have predominantly focused on museum tours, the Museum of Fine Arts, Boston, put the attention on the sales of t-shirts and mugs printed with Monet motifs, facial masks and notebooks. Basically, the museum shop went online. That inspires. However, the museum shop is not equal to the sacred halls of the museum itself. Furthermore, the museum is no longer where visitors necessarily expect an art exhibition. Extraordinary like the location of a pop-up store, the Chinese city of Changsha has turned a highly frequented metro station into a digital art museum. The museum counts six large-scale 3D LED art installations, which transform the subway commuting space into a futuristic art space.[18] Based on alternating lights, colours and animations, that installation can be continuously updated in real time. The 2000 square metres between lines 2 and 4 transform into an immersive universe with a strong sense of fashion and technology. In this metro station, art gets accessible to everyone.

Art always inspired luxury. Hence, those examples can offer new routes to reach new audiences. The close link between luxury and art is well known. Both claim for uniqueness—the ultimate level of scarcity. However, in luxury that scarcity is often an artificially created one—especially in our days of luxury democratisation. In short, art is luxury at its best. Even more, art can tell stories where words alone risk to fail.

5.1.3 Social Media and Gamification Play an Essential Role in Entertainment and Inspiration

There are new ways to connect with the younger generations and gaming is going to be a huge one. There is no doubt. (…) It would be crazy not to think about it.
—François-Henry Bennahmias CEO at Audemars Piguet, Questionnaire Conducted by the Authors

As outlined in Sect. 3.2 in Chap. 3, the smartphone in our pocket acts as a shortcut to that ultimate sense of belonging to a community. Social media are where we can find snackable content that is easy to digest and often entertaining and inspiring while the magic is rooted in the psychology behind it: people love positive feedback and rewards. Social media communities provide those in the format of likes, comments and tweets, which give us enough motivation to share our next selfie with the world. This explains the emotional addiction to social networks, which is continually evolving and is what brands use strategically to strengthen their relationship with followers. Games and gamification, smartly positioned in social networks to broaden the reach, create those desired moments of adrenaline.

For example, in 2019, Louis Vuitton partnered with Riot Games for the 'League of Legends Championship' in Paris. For that event, the artistic director Nicolas Ghesquière designed digital assets, such as new skins for the e-sport highlight, including a clothing capsule collection. That news spread through the social media channels first and attracted attention to the game itself in the second step.

As a homage to the brand's equestrian heritage, Hermès has launched a mobile gaming application called 'H-pitchhh', in which users virtually throw a horseshoe at a target.[19] All the illustrations were made with the unique Hermès look and feel, and as more credits are earned, more virtual worlds are unlocked for the user.

What these games have in common is that they represent the user through avatars embedded in a narrative. The user is empowered to communicate and interact with the community in a 3D environment. Rewards and ranks encourage the user to deal with fictive currencies and motivate him or her to compete and play against the artificial pressure generated by time limits. These time limits reinforce the non-voluntary aspect of games, leading the protagonist step by step through the experience.

Beyond storytelling and playing with brand icons, it is a proven practice to offer try-on experiences as a seamless transition to the engagement phase. The 'Sims Social' game was created as a Facebook video game extension. As a copy of real life, the game invites players to try virtual products of brands such as Moschino, Samsung and Toyota. The special highlight in this experience is that the avatar itself runs the try-on. Like in the real world, the avatar tries on fashion, accessories, watches and jewellery and pays in virtual or real currencies. That procedure acts as playful and mental preparation before the customer interacts with a product in real life. However, the digital ownership alone triggers already strong emotions, and it's not granted that a physical ownership of the product is an automatic consequence resulting out of the virtual experience. Rather than that, the game functions as a touchpoint to charge the brand perception with values.

Similar, but different, is a new type of social media network that we see with the rise of platforms like 'IMVU'. IMVU has seven million active users a month, mainly female, aged from 18 to 24. As an online metaverse, the social platform grew by 44 per cent during the pandemic.[20] Users chat, connect, design their personal avatars in 3D and dress them in clothes designed by other platform users, bought with credits paid for with real currencies. The IMVU platform operates on an open pricing model. The more than 200,000 creators claim their own prices on the 50 million digital creations that they made to inspire and to sell. The platform also leverages platforms like OpenSea for NFTs and invented its own cryptocurrency 'VCOIN' that can be exchanged on the platform to allow designers to make real money based on their digital creations. On top, users organise their own fashion shows on IMVU and form virtual model agencies. In collaboration with fashion brands, the platform released its first avatar fashion show and streamed the session on YouTube. That example shows how avatars and virtual products become a normal part of a colourful phygital life. Another example is the sales of the digital version of a Gucci Dionysus bag with bee on the Roblox marketplace

5 Digital Transformation of the Omni-personal Customer Journey

for over US$4100, exceeding the price of the physical bag at around US$3400.[21] That story is remarkable as we talk about a digital copy only. It is not an NFT, and thus, it is not transferable outside the Roblox platform, which leads to additional exclusivity for the ownership of the digital version.

In conclusion, games and gamified experiences are enjoying growing popularity, particularly among members of Gen Y and Gen Z, who grew up with digital games (Fig. 5.6). They often learned how to interact with technology through them. In addition, merging with social media enables the viral power of games and gamified experiences to be scaled. The tremendous success of that approach becomes obvious when we think about e-sport games, such as 'Pokémon Go' and 'Fortnite'.

A brand needs to have a single and clear strategic objective in mind when applying a game or gamification concept. That is true for brand-owned applications and experiences as well as for collaborations within the professional gaming industry. The user always has a fair interest in understanding the benefit quickly and easily. Mixing entertainment with brand knowledge and sales tends to be risky for a brand and counterintuitive for the user, if not executed with great perfection and experience. Therefore, the number one recommendation is to keep the concept simple and the content rich to ensure a balanced relationship between customer experience and reward. That is the best way to inspire people and stay in their mind.

Fig. 5.6 Games and gamified experiences are enjoying growing popularity, particularly among younger generations (Image: Gorodenkoff—stock.adobe.com)

5.1.4 Online Advertising Acts as a Door Opener for Websites and Online Shops

Stopping advertising to save money is like stopping your watch to save time.
—Henry Ford, Founder of the Ford Motor Company

We mentioned that the awareness phase is all about bringing prospective customers to the shop and providing an appropriate welcome ceremony to encourage them to stay there. People come into contact with brand advertising via classical magazines, exclusive events, out-of-home advertising, social media, social advertising, search engine advertising (SEA) and search results as a consequence of search engine optimisation (SEO).

Advertising for jewellery and watches targets customers' heart and brain, but typically the luxury search is emotional and brand driven and not about functional value. Certainly, people search for 'engagement rings', but a look at Google Trends tells us that a good number of searches immediately target a brand in combination with the product family or collection name, such as 'Cartier ring', with the intention of paying the brand website a direct visit.[22] That is what we refer to as direct traffic.

However, SEA and SEO are also needed in the luxury segment to protect a brand's reputation in times of counterfeiting and to stand out against the competition from other brands and the wholesale channel, which is only one mouse click away. It is a natural interest of a brand for its official brand website to remain at the top of brand-related search results, whether paid for or captured organically.

Paid advertising on affiliate websites or as part of remarketing campaigns needs to be carefully monitored. One day you have seen that mind-blowing visual of Audemars Piguet's 'Grande Sonnerie' and immediately fallen in love with it. Next time you search for Audemars Piguet's 'Grande Sonnerie', you find the remarketing campaign following you through the Web. That is fine as long as contextual cues, like the logo, claim and colours, are consistently used to recall your personal memory. Besides, an advertisement should never appear in a moral contradiction due to its placement location, for instance a provocative luxury ad next to a world hunger aid ad, so exclusion and inclusion lists need to be actively managed. They prevent a brand name appearing in a misleading context and avoid competitors bidding on brand-owned keywords. That implies registering the trademark with Google Ads to ensure that others cannot bid on the brand name, its collection and its iconic product names.

In the end, SEO is just a different kind of paid visibility. We tend to think about Google first, but that is region specific, and depending on the target geography, we should not forget about Bing, Yahoo, Baidu or Yandex. Regardless of the search engine used, there are various options to increase the SEO ranks artificially—always considering that each search engine has its own algorithm to rank the results displayed. Literally, being on top always comes at a price. In reverse, the free search is at risk as brand visibility depends on algorithms. Those algorithms are continuously improving to differentiate the real benefit for the website visitor from a simulated one. At the end of the day, there is no workaround to replace true added value and usability. In respect of SEO, expert blogs and online encyclopaedia answering frequently asked questions on jewellery, timepieces, gemstones and diamonds are an intelligent way to increase the organic search share sustainably, given that the content is unique and relevant for the visitor. Start a search for the 4 Cs of diamonds and find Tiffany's 'The Guide to Diamonds'.

Additionally, referral links from affiliate partners or social media advertising count in welcoming prospective customers to the brand universe. Social media platforms create an inviting and more social variant of a search engine. How many people go directly to Pinterest and Instagram to search for inspiration instead of looking at Google Images? Brands such as A. Lange & Söhne are managing to tempt their users on WeChat to leave their contact details so that they can receive the latest brand news. Similarly, Swarovski includes calls to action in its welcome journey, redirecting users to its loyalty programme and store locator.

Once a person has entered an online shop, the first impression matters to keep his or her attention. Does the landing page has a luxurious look and feel? Does it meet the customer's need? An inspiring campaign micro-page is not expected when searching for product details and the availability of a certain item. A product detail page is not needed when looking for a category page to be inspired by different collections. The content displayed needs to refer to the brand promise given in the advertising or SEO page title to answer the questions of what and why and to prevent the user leaving the page due to irrelevant information.

From page accessibility across devices and browsers through intuitive navigation to layout and content consistency, usability is vital to control the website's appearance to the visitor. Beyond the expected, our brain is always looking for the distinction to capture our attention; this is also known as the Von Restorff effect.[23] The trigger is extraordinary wording, a surprising call to action or an interactive element positioned directly after the page has loaded. In the case that certain areas of the Web page should attract special attention, an arrow-like arrangement of contents or the line of sight of depicted persons helps to target the desired purpose. That effect consequently reduces the bounce rates. In other words, the show can begin.

In summary, it makes no difference whether customers are on- or offsite. The rules of visibility are set and the limits of the possible are defined by platforms: search engines, social media networks and advertising portals. As long as you do not land a viral super hit, you pay to be at the top. That is not a bad deal in times of chronic information overload and omni-present distraction.

5.2 Inspire Engagement to Be Relevant to Purchase Decisions

Imagine that you follow Chopard actively on Instagram and regularly like and comment on what you see. Since the launch of the Instagram Shopping extension, you also open the tagged items in the images to see their prices and access complete product information via the linked detail pages. Your companion asks you to go on the Audemars Piguet website and open the store locator to satisfy his 'where to buy' curiosity. Alternatively, your mother agrees to be contacted monthly and exclusively via e-mail by her favourite brand for brand news and events. When opening her personalised newsletter, she receives an invitation from her sales associate to a preview of the new collection. It is up to her to choose between an in-store event and a virtual reality store appointment. Arriving in the store, she is invited to look at selected pieces of the new collection. As a special add-on, she takes the chance to try on historical jewellery creations with a digital mirror. Finally, Bulgari enables customers, through its invitation-only app, to try on the Barocko collection virtually.

Once people have entered the brand universe and they know who you are and vice versa, they proceed to the engagement phase, in which the brand needs to convince them and eliminate their last remaining doubts. The ultimate target of that phase is to lead seamlessly into a sales ceremony. The art in luxury is to avoid pressure in that step and give the individual the time, space and freedom necessary to focus emotionally on the dream and desire for a certain piece of art. The aim behind product and brand engagement is to make the dream of complete or at least temporary ownership a tangible one even if it implies that some people will need their lifelong savings to afford the desired creation.

5.2.1 In-Store Innovation Is an Invitation for Brand and Product Interaction

Monsieur Cartier and Mademoiselle Chanel remembered who they had talked to and who had tried on their latest creations. They realised when certain persons asked for the same artwork twice. They connected the dots, resulting in the right words at a good moment. The founders created a way to surprise because they knew their customer preferences by heart and were driven by innovation in design.

Nowadays, we extend this understanding towards innovation in design and experience. The need to surprise the customer is tackled by pop-up store experiences but also increasingly by flagship and classical stores, known as pop-in stores. These stores call for flexibility and openness to frequent and scalable innovations. They are an invitation for customers to engage in phygital and immersive product interaction. The traditional store experience is embedded into an omni-channel context by adding digital technologies like streaming and broadcasting, smart screens, radio-frequency identification (RFID), QR codes, iBeacon and GPS to unlock new experiences.

Streaming, Broadcasting and Co-browsing
Cross-channel events appear as one of those experiences. Just think about a virtual store visit in which the customer books a Skype, Zoom, FaceTime or Samesurf co-browsing appointment with his or her personal sales associate, who leads via video broadcast with a 360-degree experience. The customer, in real time, follows a guided tour through the boutique and its creations. High-resolution cameras, videos and digital twins or even virtual boutiques visualise what would otherwise only be experienceable in store. Using the example of the watchmaker Hublot, the customer selects upfront the three most interesting timepieces, and the sales associate prepares all the relevant material for the virtual ceremony. Cartier offers a similar service, presenting the pieces worn on real models and involving experts' talk,[24] and private broadcasts have become the tool of choice to connect with VIP customers. The brand teamed up with the creative agency Prodject to create a unique experience by blending filmmaking and art performance with marketing. Nothing was left to chance: to recreate the catering experience, guests received a gift box beforehand to pair the experience with champagne, caviar and chocolate.[25] Obviously, those high-end experiences are designed for VIPs. Returning to the sales ceremony at scale, brands like Piaget and IWC have started to offer virtual store appointments with sales associates. For a one-to-one session,

platforms like Hero, Beehivr, Inspify, Lode and Bambuser provide solutions, although the latter is also applicable in a one-to-many streaming context. In that case, the streaming window is embedded directly in a brand website to generate qualified leads in a brand-owned and brand-controlled environment. In contrast, streams hosted on third-party platforms, like Tmall and JD, benefit more from the access to a broad platform user base. In addition, Accenture provides a virtual showcase platform with e-commerce, CRM and analytics integration, unlocking customer engagement in a one-to-one and one-to-many set-up (Fig 5.7).[26]

Smart Screens
Whether in store or through a window, digital walls, mirrors, tables and tablets can be used to share brand knowledge playfully. There is a huge variety of smart touchscreen formats, but the screen just enables the experience. In the jewellery and watch context, gemmology, watchmaking expertise, style advisors, brand origin, historical creations, royal customers, iconic creations or sustainability insights provide inspiration to build a strong narrative around the brand's uniqueness, embedding games, quizzes or competitions. The engagement effect accelerates with motion control add-ons like the 'Leap Motion Controller' by Ultraleap, which empowers passers-by to interact with the screen through hand gestures, as well as the engagement factor, which is of course also a strong awareness builder.

For instance, smart mirrors facilitate catalogue browsing and augment the virtual trying on of creations that are currently not in the inventory; they are

Fig. 5.7 Virtual showcase platform, Accenture, 2021 (Printed with Accenture's permission)

offered for instance by Prada, Rebecca Minkoff, Ralph Lauren, Helzberg Diamonds and the Chinese high-end jewellery retailer Chow Sang Sang. Even the trying on of multiple pieces at the same time has been demonstrated by the fine jewellery brand Djula.[27] The brands work with connected fitting rooms, including a smart mirror.[28] Thanks to the RFID chip attached to each product, the mirror recognises the items brought to the fitting room. Furthermore, additional product details, variants and sizes can be displayed in different languages based on the individual customer's preference. The lighting mood in the fitting room simulates various settings between morning and evening. Moreover, all these customer preferences are tracked by the smart mirror—together with data about the length of the session or the conversion rate. These data enable business analysts to aggregate valuable insights and to make better decisions to personalise the interaction further. Displaying the user's name to welcome the visitor in a more personal way gives every experience a positive starting point.

In addition, social media integrations can extend digital mirrors, walls or tables. The Helzberg Virtual Ring Experience, for instance, uses motion sensors to display rings on the hand of a user from different angles and allows pictures to be taken while doing so. These pictures are immediately shareable through social media or e-mail.

In general, neither smart mirrors nor digital walls should act as a self-service tool but should always be embedded in the in-store ceremony and communication with the sales associate. The sales associate guides the customer through the experience and assists when another colour, size or material variant is requested. He or she ensures the personal link and mitigates the risk of the customer being blocked by technical constraints. A customer should never feel alone in that experience, as long as he or she did not ask to be.

QR Codes

With the support of a smartphone, QR codes act as a shortcut between brand, product and customer. It takes one scan to connect the customer with product details or to encourage the usage of digital warranty cards. The relevant QR codes are, for example, printed on the warranty cards or follow a pure digital approach. Brands also position QR codes in stores to establish relationships by connecting the sales associate and the customer on social media platforms like WeChat to create qualified followers. QR codes are printed for reference and given for free to prospective customers who have not yet bought anything but are showing significant interest in a certain creation. The QR technology itself does not call for additional marketing investment, but of course, the clear vision on the customer journey is the key to training sales associates appropriately. In the best case, the QR codes in store drive traffic to the website and the website drives revenue to stores. It should also not be forgotten that QR codes positioned in a physical store window allow traffic to be rerouted to the website 24/7, offering independence from the classical opening hours of a physical store.

iBeacon and GPS

Apple has introduced iBeacon as a positioning technology. It refers to a protocol standard for Bluetooth low-energy sensing based on a unique identifier. It allows devices to be located in store or nearby, given that the necessary application has been installed on the device upfront. With its installation, the user agrees to the terms and conditions and gives the legally required consent to be contacted via the mobile application. Once confirmed, iBeacon allows the customer's movement paths to be monitored and push notifications or social media actions to be triggered based on the mobile device's location, which is an interesting way to grant VIP treatment to the customer. The user just needs to pass close enough to an iBeacon transmitter, and a signal is sent to the user device. All user data, such as indoor positioning and product interaction, are stored on the mobile application and not on the iBeacon transmitter, which provides the user with further data security. Extensions to mobile marketing, commerce and touchless payment via Apple Pay are possible. Different from GPS tracking, the iBeacon device location is more precise and less energy intense.

In short, technologies unlock new experiences, such as cross-channel events, interactive learning, virtual trying on and in-store VIP treatments. Moreover, the tracking of customer behaviour and paths gives insights into the optimal store layout and product positioning. Still, it is never about high-tech; it is purely about guaranteeing high-touch.

5.2.2 The Webmosphere and Relevant Online Features Drive Action

> *E-commerce is the fastest-growing channel in the luxury industry, but it is not only a channel on top of the existing ones (wholesale, retail, travel retail). It is not anymore the cherry on the cake, but it is becoming the cake, especially when it is about the net results and equity.*
>
> —Antonio Carriero, Chief Digital and Technology Officer of Breitling, Questionnaire Conducted by the Authors

Nearly every second offline purchase action has been prepared through online engagement,[29] also called the ROPO effect: research online, purchase offline. That illustrates the importance of the online presence and the brand website as the first address on the Web. There is no doubt that the visual aesthetics of luxury websites need to appear brand consistent. All the love of details and product excellence need to be omnipresent across channels. Besides a luxurious webmosphere and the knowledge about behavioural patterns, interaction and experience in an omni-personal sense need to be unlocked on the brand's website and in its respective online shop.

Responsive AI Web Design
Your shop remembers you. Last time, you browsed the online shop for rose-gold rings. When reopening the storefront, rose-gold rings welcome you back into the store. With responsive AI Web design, the content blocks and layout of a website or storefront adjust dynamically in real time. The crux of AI Web design is that it always requires the customer to be known already via cookies or login to be welcomed by name. The jewellery brand Chaumet, for example, elegantly embeds the customer name into its 'Inimitable Joséphine' micro-page, the virtual visit of the 12 Vendôme Hotel Particulier. When entering the experience, the brand asks visitors for their name, which is remembered and displayed later in the digital ceremony.[30]

In general, preferences identified based on customers' wish list, sales history, mobile application usage and other information are used to segment customers via tools like a CDP and to personalise the displayed content. Mood boards aim to reflect the individual style and collection preferences.

A lady who is in love with Harry Winston's 'Secret' collection will appreciate seeing the latest interpretation of the 'Secret' earrings on her personalised landing page but probably only as long as the creation is on her wish list and she does not already own the desired one. If she has bought the earrings, she is likely to be more interested in the matching necklace. In the case that her companion has bought the earrings as a gift for her, this matters only if she or he has shared that information with the brand. Loyalty programmes and digital passports are a way to track the ownership complexities involved in gift purchases. Otherwise, the brand risks promoting an item that has already been successfully sold, and that translates into missed potential. This example is thought to highlight the importance of setting the right filters in AI Web design and taking the shared customer data into account for ongoing optimisation. In front of your customer, you should be up to date, knowing the common sales and wish list history.

Website Features

Certain features are expected on a luxury website to merge the on- and offline environments into one seamless experience. The search for collections, iconic products, store locations and brand values should be, in any case, a quick one. As an advanced feature, a visual search tool, such as the one by Forevermark (Fig. 5.8), can enrich the journey. In addition, product detail pages need to provide exhaustive product information, including rich content such as high-resolution images, videos and 360-degree views. In addition, the click-and-collect feature creates a user-friendly way to reserve an item in store based on the customer-selected location. The wish list offers an easy way to prepare purchase decisions. Moreover, it enables indirect product comparisons, which are not seen as a stand-alone feature in the luxury segment.

We agree that artwork is incomparable. Art needs to be presented, admired, appreciated, celebrated, desired and finally requested. That is why many high-end jewellery and watch brands avoid 'buy' buttons on their website and add 'price on request' remarks for pieces above entry level. The call to action ranges from 'find a store', 'request now' or 'book an appointment' to 'click to try', 'virtual try on' or 'order by phone'. The simple reason behind this is to protect the personal link and provide a luxurious sales ceremony. Individuals love the personal appreciation and recognition that they experience during the

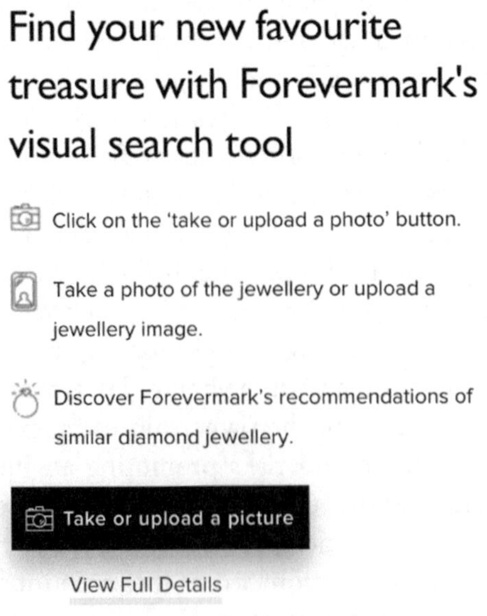

Find your new favourite treasure with Forevermark's visual search tool

- Click on the 'take or upload a photo' button.
- Take a photo of the jewellery or upload a jewellery image.
- Discover Forevermark's recommendations of similar diamond jewellery.

[Take or upload a picture]

View Full Details

Fig. 5.8 Visual search tool, Forevermark, 2021 (Printed with Forevermark's permission)

presentation of an art creation, independent of their culture, generation and age. Nevertheless, younger generations are used to purchasing online, and keeping them in the queue of requesters for too long is a surprising and painful experience that demands their patience. The risk here is that, while they are waiting, they will fall in love with a more accessible substitute and opt for it, while former generations would have continued waiting until the dream came true. Hence, it is important to rethink the way in which creations are presented online—not only for certain entry collections but also for certain customer segments.

Virtual Agents

While virtual or conversational agents and chatbots are considered as interesting performance optimisers for internal communication in luxury, they are not viewed as appropriate for end-client facing communication at that stage—in particular for emotion-engaging and explanation-intense interaction. The customer relationship is too valuable as an asset to put it at risk in an automated communication, which may not appear to be personal or relevant enough. For pure information and admin-related requests, such as 'Where is my invoice' or 'Tell me the opening hours of the Zenith store in Zurich' or even for step by step product configuration, the application of virtual agents and chatbots is supposed to unlock efficiencies as they are available 24/7 and never out of office. Still, the key challenge is to identify the right moment at which the conversation stream needs to be handed over to a human agent. The new generation of social virtual agents is designed to overcome this challenge based on artificial intelligence, semantic analysis and natural language processing (NLP). That also applies in the luxury context, but a certain amount of time is necessary to train the algorithm—also in regard to brand-congruent tonality and multilingualism. Online live chats managed by human agents appear to be less critical, but here as well, keeping the impression of immediate service availability is not easy with increasing numbers of conversations and a lack of scalability. Despite the increasing number of virtual appointments, for many brands, phone calls remain the preferred contact channel as they grant a personal touch and control.

Appointment Booking

Like virtual agents, appointment-booking tools never sleep. Despite that, the tools just support humans; they do not take over their job. Web-based systems, such as Timify or SimplyBook.me, embed appointment-booking functionality into the website. Both tools lead customers through the process step by step: choose the appointment date, the sales associate and the time slot; process user authentication; and receive the booking confirmation straight away as a calendar entry via e-mail (Fig. 5.9). Reminder mails are often triggered 24 hours and 30 minutes before the scheduled appointment, including a preview of the session, an appointment edit option or technical advice on how to guarantee the best user experience. Appointment-booking tools are in high demand these days—not least because of the COVID-19 situation and the visitor restrictions faced in store. They offer an easy and intuitive way to connect one to one with the customer.

Virtual Try-On
In Sect. 5.1.1, we outlined AR and VR applications as a way to display products from a new perspective. Beyond that, AR applications allow new ways to interact with a product, such as virtual product try-on. Thanks to augmented reality, customers can visualise in a playful way how jewellery or watches would look on their own wrist, neck or ear. This is what J*Art, an AI-based mobile and Web image recognition product, developed by Moqod, is offering. However, there are several providers with a focus on jewellery and watches, including Tryon and Quytech, to mention a couple.

Virtual try-on applications show huge potential to make the digital sales ceremony more interactive and appropriate for the individual (Fig. 5.10). Still, for the time being, these applications have certain limitations. The

Fig. 5.9 Appointment-booking tool, Courbet, 2021 (Printed with Courbet's permission)

Fig. 5.10 Virtual try-on applications show huge potential to make the digital sales ceremony more interactive (Image: Andrey Popov—stock.adobe.com)

challenges involve the precise positioning of the item, the rendering time, compatibility across operating systems and the fact that some applications work with picture input only.

In the case that an AI solution is too complex to answer one of the key questions in life—how to find the right ring size—a simplified approach is available. Tested over Valentine's Day in China, Chaumet has launched its WeChat smart size guide mini programme to measure finger sizes in 360 degrees. In that solution, the user puts a finger on the mobile device, and bars on the right and left measure the diameter of the finger at different reference points. Based on a calculation, the ring size is identified. This approach requires no AR and complex AI but is less engaging and shareable in social networks.

Virtual Stores

Virtual stores started when Burberry had the visionary idea of converting the classical runway into a digital event. The idea of real-time brand–customer interaction in a phygital set-up was born. Today, not only can complete fashion week events be enjoyed virtually, but the whole store can be transformed into a virtual place, reaching far beyond what is possible in a traditional store. Virtual reality stores are made to open new worlds for immersive experiences. Virtual reality becomes a brand universe itself, only limited by creativity and the human power of imagination. In a virtual store, jewellery can fly around freely as physical laws like gravity no longer restrict it. Watches can change colour and shape to display the available variants in an endless fluid metamorphosis. The customer builds part of a narrative in co-creation with the brand. You look into the mirror and meet historical customers to talk with them about iconic creations. You become a pilot targeting the sky; looking at your wrist, the timepiece tells you the time. You dive into a shipwreck and check the time on your Luminor. We are no longer observers of heroes. We want to be part of the story—creating our own story with a brand. That is the priceless dream of the Now. From pure consumption, we take the road to co-creation. The sales associate acts as a virtual concierge on that journey, and the geographic location of the sales associate or the customer no longer matters. All that is needed is a stable Internet connection. In other words, a customer with a home town of Geneva can connect with his or her personal concierge in Geneva for a virtual store visit even when staying on a remote island in the Indian Ocean. The customer is empowered to connect with the brand representative, knowing him or her best.

Avatars as animated characters support all the social interaction in that brand universe. They chat and share, act and react, move and collaborate with other avatars. Finally, at the moment of forcing ourselves back into reality, we leave with strong emotions and even stronger dreams of returning soon to begin a new adventure. Technology-wise, the virtual showroom providers Obsess and Lode have shown special expertise in the luxury context. Clearly, we can expect more to come.

To sum up, the luxurious webmosphere alone is not sufficient to trigger customer action on the website. It is important to activate user-relevant online features to engage with the customer. Responsive AI Web design, wish lists, customised appointments in the physical or virtual store and even the usage of avatars further personalise the experience. Beyond the website and Web shop, the whole marketing ecosystem, including social media and social commerce (see Sect. 3.2. in Chap. 3), acts as an engaging extension to bring the webmosphere into the mind of customers. In fact, that is independent of the device and the content format: from product visuals over videos to voice content.

5.2.3 Influencer Marketing and How Rich Content Seeds Dreams

The achievement of our time is that the brand monologue has changed into a dialogue: the brand inspires followers, and the followers inspire the brand. They engage with the community and create user-generated content. When brand followers reach more people with their content, they transform into influencers. In other words, they evolve into professional marketing partners for a brand. Influencers are paid with sample products and money to embed advertising in their channel, to share their opinion in the format of picture posts, blogs and vlogs or even to act as a brand ambassador. Ambassadors act exclusively as the brand's face within a certain time frame. In the past, that was a privilege for royals, outstanding sportspeople and Hollywood stars. Nowadays, the barriers have become more fluid. Little girls do not necessarily dream of one day becoming a princess any longer. The new dream is to become a successful businesswoman—beautiful, autonomous and with the freedom to travel wherever they want. That could match the profile of a successful influencer. Becoming a brand ambassador is no longer mission impossible.

Brands like Tiffany and Bulgari have shown successfully how an engaging hashtag can be leveraged to encourage user-generated content. The Tiffany campaign #LoveNotLike on Snapchat in 2016 triggered a playful selfie creation hype in which brand icons inspired users' creativity. Buccellati collaborated with Noonoouri, a digital model and influencer with roughly 400,000 followers on Instagram. Balenciaga created a science-fiction inspired runway leveraging a digital twin of the model Elisa Douglas for the launch of its new SP22 collection. Breguet worked with local influencers to target watch enthusiasts in Taiwan and the Philippines.[31] All these examples highlight the strong relationship between luxury brands and influencers, unified in the common objective of generating rich, engaging content.

5.2.4 Clienteling Is Bringing the Communication to the Next Level

Monsieur Cartier wrote paper-based invitation letters to his VIP customers. Nothing has changed since then. Luxury VIP customers still receive handwritten letters from their personal sales associate. That is an amazing method of personalisation and is perceived as even more luxurious in a world where handwriting itself is becoming a rare luxury. However, there are certain constraints, such as the readability, efficiency and scalability of that communication. That is where digitally supported and enabled communication is a must-have extension for luxury brands to offer seamless engagement.

How can brands ensure that the information provided is relevant to the individual? How can they avoid spamming their fans and followers with one-directional mass communication? How can they guarantee that the communication resonates with the customers' interest, resulting in emotions and actions?

CRM clienteling extensions, like the solutions provided by Salesforce and Microsoft, answer these questions, and the start-up Seer offers a mobile app to create personalised content in a luxurious magazine style that is shareable with clients via social media platforms such as WeChat and e-mail. In general, clienteling describes the capturing of customers' personal preferences regarding products, contact channels, shopping occasion and frequency, average basket size and special interests, including their wish list and hobbies. The sales associate enters those data via a mobile app in store, or the customer himself or herself gives an online shop the necessary details to increase the relevance of the interactions. Or to quote Antonio Carriero, Chief Digital and Technology Officer of Breitling:

> *Clienteling is the art of engaging with the customer, across any channel and media, physically or digitally. Clienteling is at the heart of Retail, Connected Retail and we are Connected Retailers. We build long term relations with our customers based on the value we share with them, and of course the products!*

A clienteling solution provides features for business analysts, marketing and commerce managers, boutique managers and sales associates. It enables the identification of behaviour patterns and the clustering into customer segments, such as VIP customers, watch and jewellery enthusiasts, frequent customers, prospective customers, brand novices, followers of certain collections, and category-exclusive or customer service customers only. Of course, the appropriate segmentation is defined by the brand. For those segments, different communication strategies and objectives are defined to target marketing campaigns better. Moreover, users can apply several filters to obtain, for instance, a ranked view of the top-ten VIP customers of a certain store. Further added value is granted by the embedding of the product catalogue, event and appointment management features, e-mail and social media integration or analytics with aggregated views on KPIs.

The basic requirement for clienteling is first and foremost that the customer has been registered upfront, which typically occurs via one of the three available channels: in store (retail and wholesale), on the website (e-commerce) and on social media (marketing). In return for the registration, the customer receives personalised services, such as birthday surprises, a welcome ceremony by name, event invitations or newsletters. The second requirement is that all the customer data captured in different databases by channel, regional authorisation group and brand are merged into one common database. That aggregated holistic view of the customer is also called the golden record. Finally, the third requirement is that the user is recognised and trackable in the channel. In the store, the customer mentions his name. Online, the customer is identified via the login or cookies. Marketing automation systems track every visit and action. However, they cannot control what happens when users are not logged in and use different IP addresses as they interact across devices. That causes data inaccuracy, which needs to be considered.[32]

Let us be more visual: recently, one of our authors received an e-mail from his personal Tiffany sales associate. It was written in the tonality of a good friend, reaching out to ask about his and his family's well-being. In addition, the sales associate outlined that she had been thinking about him and would be happy to hear from him. In the last note, she shared her best wishes for his upcoming wedding anniversary. Only the Tiffany name in the signature and e-mail address indicated the link to the brand and suggested a deeper intention: prompting thoughts about an anniversary present for his companion. The personal conclusion that a piece of Tiffany jewellery would be just right, since the wedding ring came from the same brand, remained up to the customer. Of course, the sales associate had a CDP and clienteling tool to remind her of the wedding anniversary. We consider this as an excellent use case to show how e-mail marketing based on clienteling enables highly personal and brand-consistent communication and unlocks new potential.

E-mail marketing is only one channel in which clienteling makes a big difference. Beyond it, there are various use cases: earlier in this book, we considered appointment booking and VR product presentations. It is self-explanatory that a clienteling tool brings valuable insights for experience personalisation. The sales associate checks the customer segment, sales history and customer preferences before the VR session to design a relevant experience. Another example is the consideration of customer segments to optimise content for social media channels like WeChat. It is no surprise that content that matches the individual customer preferences performs better and reduces marketing costs significantly. It does not imply recreating the content from scratch but helps to adjust details of the wording or positioning.[33]

5.3 Trigger Conversion to Achieve Customer Satisfaction

For her special birthday, your partner would like a Reverso watch from Jaeger-LeCoultre. You visit the boutique together to configure the watch, make the purchase, join the loyalty programme and adjust the bracelet to make sure that it fits perfectly. Your sales associate shares his expertise and gives helpful watch care instructions. Browsing the Chopard online shop, you stop once again at the 'Happy Diamonds' collection to add the iconic ring with the dancing diamond to your cart. It is simply the perfect match for your Happy Diamonds watch and necklace. Recently you have been promoted, and the Chopard ring is still on your wish list. You receive an e-mail reminder and think it is a good time for some self-rewarding. Last but not least, your friend is looking for an engagement ring. He is less brand conscious than his beloved. However, he knows that the ring is supposed to be from Cartier. To find the perfect engagement ring, he books a virtual sales appointment.

The rational target in this phase is sales. The emotional target is excitement and satisfaction once the transaction has been completed. In this phase, each detail matters because one thing is certain: the customer will buy only when absolutely convinced. As long as there is still a perceived risk that is stronger than the purchase desire, the easiest solution is to postpone the purchase decision. That behaviour is rooted in our human nature: decisions create tensions. Tensions activate our instincts, in the worst case the instinct to escape. A good sales associate is aware of these behavioural patterns and realises when the customer needs time or reassuring arguments to make a purchase decision (Fig. 5.11).[34] Due to the price points in jewellery and watches, evaluating the investment carefully is an important and highly personal process.

5.3.1 In-Store Product and Service Personalisation Calls for an Upgrade

In-store product and service personalisation bridges the engagement with the conversion phase. Monsieur Cartier and Mademoiselle Chanel offered personalised service and custom-made creations to their VIP customers. That is nothing new to luxury, but the extension of those special treatments towards broader customer segments is definitely new. This is what is happening now when we think about product configuration tools, 3D printing and the consideration of preferred check-out channels and payment preferences.

5 Digital Transformation of the Omni-personal Customer Journey   99

	RECURRENT OCCASION	**UNIQUE OCCASION**
Familiar to the brand	**Online Sales** for a follow-up or product update purchase with high brand knowledge	**Online or In-Store Sales** for a special occasion with high brand knowledge
New to the brand	**Online or In-Store Sales** for a rational best-in-class purchase with low brand knowledge	**In-Store Sales** for a special occasion such as birthday or anniversary with low brand knowledge

Fig. 5.11 Overview of sales scenarios

Check-Out Preferences

In the case that a product is not available in store but the customer is convinced by his or her choice, the click from store omni-channel scenario should be activated. That allows the end customer to order the desired creation in store for in-store pick-up or home delivery. Of course, the other way around is also common practice in today's world: ordering the item online and picking it up in store. This scenario is known as click and collect. Whether a sale occurs in the store or online, its declaration leads to the activation of the guarantee. In the case of watches, this warranty period is generally two years.

From a psychological point of view, the warranty activation gives finality to the purchase and reassures the customer about the after-sales service. In this way, the risk of returns can already be sustainably reduced during the sale. However, even more important than a reassuring warranty is the pre-purchase research and the interaction between sales associate and customer across digital and physical spaces. Typically, a hard luxury purchase asks for intense upfront research. You search online, visit the store for advice, try on, look online once again and try on for a second time and even a third time before making a purchase decision. This is a sample customer journey, but the warranty does not replace it. Finally, that intense research and engagement phase is the best way to prevent product returns, at least as long as the purchase is not motivated by the 'wear it only once before returning it' mentality.

Payment Preferences
The super-rich royals of the past rarely touched money themselves. They had servants to manage payments on their behalf. Credit card payments create a method to decouple the pain of payment from the pleasure of purchase. Only the positive should be permanently anchored in the customer's memory. This becomes even more effective when removing the physical payment counter from the store and replacing it with a smart check-out solution. As a pioneer, Apple has demonstrated how this works. Each floor is equipped with a separate Wi-Fi-based hub. Employees connect to that hub with their iPads to unlock mobile electronic payments via Apple Pay or a credit card or bank card. Brands are reacting to the predominant usage of Alipay and WeChat Pay among Chinese customers with extended mobile payment options to address those preferences too. The only exception to the smart check-out remains cash payment as it still requires a centralised cash register. Another option to remove the pain of physical payment is the payment via AfterPay or Klarna or the click-and-collect scenario, in which the customer pays online before picking up the creation from the store. Last but not least, the subscription model completely disconnects the payment from the happy moment of receiving a creation in a gift-like emotional set-up. The best gift is the one that you present to yourself.

In-Store Product Configuration
A personalised product configuration experience is entertaining and triggers co-creation. As mentioned earlier in this book (Sect. 2.2.1 in Chap. 2), the labour-love effect explains the emotional connection to an item that requires active involvement. Product configuration tools or name-engraving simulations give us an impression of what a product will look like when it is ours. That effect is strengthened by VR tools that provide photo-realistic visualisation and animation of the final creation. Brands like Ferrari and Hermès use the convincing power of personalised configuration in their stores. Product configurators have been used in the automotive industry to map the product complexity of a new car. Often the customer has already made his or her own configuration on the home computer before fine-tuning the details with the sales associate in the store. That makes a lot of sense for items that need to be explained. Nevertheless, luxury creations of all kinds benefit from visual simulation that is as close to reality as possible. Besides the pleasant anticipation and thrill, it helps to reduce cancellation and return rates. In addition, personalised products are usually excluded from the possibility of being returned.

Brands like Burberry and Louis Vuitton have launched monogram services, and Hermès introduced its 'Custom Silk Corner' initiative in 2011 to allow customers to co-create unique scarves. That service was available exclusively in selected stores.

While in-store product configurators are perceived as being nice to have as they support the physical product presentation, they become a clear necessity in the online channel. An online shop without the possibility of trying a product on virtually or using a product configurator is missing a solid argument, showing how the product fits into your world and suits your personality. Why are you confident about using the positive momentum to buy now online and not later in store? Product configurators nurture an essential characteristic of luxury: uniqueness in a sense that the customer has the impression that the product is fully personalised for him or her. Technically speaking, the product configurator leads the user step by step through a decision tree to retrieve the most appropriate product recommendation from a product catalogue. From a brand point of view, it is a relatively easy and inexpensive way to give all its customers the ultimate VIP feeling. In fact, it is a smart search tool, enriched by free-text engraving—often limited to certain fonts and characters. In summary, product configurators make the expensive high-end emotion of personalised tailor-made items an affordable pleasure at scale. When a configurator leads to a recommendation, the customer feels respected and personally involved in the decision.

5.3.2 An Online Shop Is a Playful and Creative Place Where Products and Services Are Configured

Online Product Configuration

An online shop without the simulation of the final item is facing an impossible mission. People are creative regarding the details, but their creativity needs to be nurtured with colour, style, size and material information. They want to turn a 3D item to the left and right, up and down, to see the masterpiece from different angles. People want to explore, and they want to co-create the item in its perfect configuration. Perfect is not perfect from a pure brand perspective. Perfect is perfect in the customer's eyes. Otherwise, he or she will not buy.

Baume was a sub-brand of Baume and Mercier, targeting young generations—namely digital natives. The collection focuses on sustainable materials, minimalist design and personalisation, and is available online only. Before the eco-responsible brand officially joined Baume and Mercier in 2020, Baume maintained its own website and online shop, including a 3D product configurator. Like the product configurator of the French jewellery brand Courbet (Fig. 5.12), Baume's configurator was built with the Apviz Software as a Service (SaaS) platform provided by Hapticmedia, which is compatible across

Fig. 5.12 Online product finder, Courbet, 2021 (Printed with Courbet's and Hapticmedia's permission)

systems and browsers as a Web application.[35] Alternatively, configure–price–quote (CPQ) providers like Verenia or eRep are options, depending on the brand needs. The Baume solution contained 2200 available watch designs, structured in configuration sections for dial style and colour, case colour, hand style, strap material and colour, and personalised engravings. The brand followed new rules to address its target audience online by providing an engaging and playful configuration experience.

The situation is different for established brands like Rolex or Ferrari: both provide an advanced online product finder that is basically a product configuration without an online ordering feature but with a wish list feature and 'Send to dealer' option to prepare the purchase action cognitively. Step by step, the user identifies his or her favourite configuration based on style, collection, model, material, bezel and dial or respective paintwork, wheels and callipers, bodywork elements, exhaust pipes and so on. In the final step, the user searches for the nearest partner store.

Prices Online

Several watches and jewellery brands make only entry products available for online ordering up to a predefined price limit. Above that price, the call to action moves to 'Schedule Appointment' and similar engagement actions. When displaying prices, it is important to notice that, in the luxury context, it is always recommended to start with the full price, including all the modular features. With that price anchor, the customer will downscale the item features. The bottom line is that this approach leads to greater willingness to pay higher prices than the reverse approach of upgrading a basic product configuration.[36] To put it more visually, by default, the Daytona in its platinum version puts a price anchor in the visitor's mind. That anchor gives the impression that the gold version is affordable and the stainless steel version is even perhaps not enough. In the best case, we decide for the middle option, which is the gold version in our example. That example just serves to illustrate the principle. For the same reason, it makes sense to position a broad selection of high-priced references on a category page and sort them into descending order of price. That supports an exclusive appearance, and of course, the 'price on request' label fuels the myth of the unaffordable.

Deep Dive: 3D Printing

Within the last years, 3D printing has often been seen as the key to unlocking production limitations of unique creations at scale. Certainly, it is a paradox between, on the one hand, industrialisation and, on the other hand, real-time, made-to-order uniqueness—and the fact that we risk losing the 'hand-made' connection to jewellery. That even leads to fundamental questions like the one concerning the real authorship of luxury. Is it about the designer? Is it about the design? Is it about the involvement of the owner? Is it about the personal reference to the owner? 3D printing unquestionably opens the possibility of new interpretations of luxury.

Interestingly, the rising degree of digitisation among 3D printing value chains is leading to an increasing number of cases, which evidence its potential for scale. For the time being, the economic viability of 3D printing is highly dependent on the industry and the field of application. In hard luxury, 3D printing is reserved for certain materials and application areas in which prototypes or single spare parts do not achieve profitable volumes for mass production.

Based on the principle that a 3D printer can manufacture any kind of shape, the so-called freedom of design becomes a paradigm shift for designers, who can explore unseen shapes. Additionally, the capability of creating anything from the print leads to the introduction of greater individualisation of objects. This is also a notable addition for art creations as we see them in luxury watch and jewellery making but also in creating casting moulds for futuristic and delicate shapes.

Fashion designers like Iris van Herpen were among the pioneers experimenting with the new possibilities of 3D printing. Among the watchmakers, Officine Panerai started to print titanium watch frames to reduce the weight of watches by 40 per cent.[37] Italian jewellery brands like Bijouets and Maison 203 built their differentiation strategy on the new variety of shapes unlocked by 3D printing technologies (Fig. 5.13).

The French start-up Gemmyo has demonstrated how to disrupt the jewellery business model based on 3D technology: the online jeweller sells made-to-order creations only.[38] All 5500 creations in Gemmyo's online catalogue are digital twins shown for inspiration. It is up to the customer to personalise his or her favourite creation further by selecting the precious stone and metal as well as defining the size. Once the design and check-out have been completed, the 3D printing is ready to start. By coupling the Web with 3D modelling and printing, the start-up involves the customer as a co-creator in the design process—the customer satisfaction rate benefits from that customer-centric approach. At the same time, Gemmyo saves on shop rent, employee costs and inventory and storage costs for raw materials besides the expenses for admin and security.

For the time being, Stratasys and 3D Systems are the biggest providers of 3D printers and printing materials. 3D printing requires a digital source file (computer-generated 3D object), the printer and the printing materials, ranging from chocolate to resin and from plastic to metal, such as titanium, stainless steel, aluminium, gold, silver, bronze or copper.

Fig. 5.13 3D-printed jewellery, Maison 203, 2021 (Printed with Maison 203's permission)

5 Digital Transformation of the Omni-personal Customer Journey

In the watch and jewellery industry, different technologies can be applied, the most important of which are described below:

- *Fused deposition modelling (FDM)* is used to print resin or plastic prototypes or casting moulds. This technology is best for proof-of-concept and simple prototyping as it is less accurate and less expensive than alternative processes.
- *Stereolithography (SLA)* is based on UV light and adds thin material layers on top of each other to print prototypes or casting moulds with high precision and fine details. It is more expensive than FDM.
- *Direct metal laser sintering (DMLS)* technology allows 3D printing based on metal powder or granulate. It can be used to print prototypes and casting moulds, but beyond that, EOS has innovated a new DMLS process specialising in direct gold printing.[39] That process requires a certain type of granulate and laser to penetrate the metal faster than a standard laser.

Regardless of the 3D technology chosen, a jeweller or watchmaker sets precious stones into the creation and remains in charge of the final finish and polishing, including the removal of supporting constructions.

The ultimate level of product personalisation is the custom-made creation of unique pieces for an individual. Product configuration and 3D modelling support the visualisation and co-creation of the final design. From a manufacturing point of view, 3D printing technology is an innovative approach to making that dream come true affordably and promptly.

5.3.3 One e-mail Reminder Makes the Difference Between Wish List and Order

Sometimes an in-store visit and product configuration are not sufficient for customers to make a final purchase decision. Big investments need to be well thought out, and sometimes people need another night to reconsider a decision. There are two tasks for a brand: wait and remember discreetly without building up pressure and respect the individual customer's communication preferences.

In one scenario, the customer has added a reference to his or her cart or wish list without completing the check-out. There are different possible reasons for that behaviour, like an unforeseen event interrupting the purchase, missing details in the mobile version, alternative options or simply a lack of conviction to buy. Assuming that the customer has given marketing consent, a brand should not idly let the opportunity of a purchase pass by. While classic retargeting risks being perceived as too invasive, personalised e-mails gallantly remind people of forgotten references in their shopping cart or draw attention to a wish list. In the course of this, a new creation can be presented that suits the customer's individual taste better.

In another scenario, the customer lacks the physical product presentation because the desired reference is out of stock. In that case, the sales associate should ask for the customer's agreement to inform him once the reference is back in store. The follow-up communication via phone, e-mail or any other preferred contact channel can be combined with an invitation for the customer to book an appointment.

In both scenarios, the follow-up communication acts as a reminder to keep the interest in a certain creation alive and finally convert that interest into a purchase. Reminder e-mails are a personalised form of marketing communication. Probably the most important factor in that type of brand–customer communication is the right timing. As obvious as it may seem that transactional communications like order confirmations—including automatic replenishment confirmations in the B2B context—are sent to the business partner or customer immediately after the check-out, it is important to determine the best time to receive a marketing e-mail from the customer's point of view. In many companies, the fastest possible time technically still determines the sending time instead of the relevance for the customer.

5.3.4 Live Commerce Is the New Virtual Showroom

We will keep this chapter short as we have previously discussed the importance of social commerce and live streaming in China in Sect. 3.2 in Chap. 3, and in the subsequent chapter, we outlined how the new commerce format is conquering the world. We closed the chapter with a list of questions referring to its relevance for luxury brands. While the real-time aspect of live streaming and live-commerce events is certainly an advantage, the exclusive image protection remains a challenge to be overcome through ongoing innovation. The game changer is not that teleshopping is moving online but that online is moving beyond the product. At that moment, the Internet serves the brand and not the other way around. Innovative experiences protect the exclusive image of a brand. The fear of brand dilution becomes irrelevant.

5.4 Ensure Seamless Fulfilment and Exceed Customer Expectations

In an omni-personal world, you face new customer journeys. Your customer expects seamless experiences along channels and touchpoints as well as when it comes to fulfilment—order fulfilment from a brand point of view and expectation fulfilment from a customer standpoint (Fig. 5.14).

For visualisation, imagine a gentleman entering the Munich store with a special interest in a certain timepiece. He is not yet sure about buying it because he needs further time to make that decision or because the timepiece is not available in store in his dream configuration for an immediate try-on experience. First, the aspiration is that the sales associate today needs to have visibility of the inventory allocation across networks. That includes, for instance, internal and external networks and the e-com inventory, which is often managed centrally. Second, the sales associate needs to be incentivised, independently from the conversion channel. Without both, the sales associate is not necessarily encouraged to act customer centrically.

Order Management Systems

Becoming omni-channel requires the right business set-up, including legal contracts to unlock and encourage sales, independent of the sales channel. The omni-channel is about breaking with siloed structures with the ultimate objective of exploiting sales opportunities. From a customer standpoint, the sales associate should be enabled to check the inventory allocation to optimise the waiting time for the customer. Besides the improved customer experience and the maximisation of sales opportunities, the omni-channel also has positive effects on the profitability and the reduction of tied capital.

Obviously, that requires the right tools and technologies. Inventory visibility and the automatisation of processes are usually addressed with an order management system (OMS), which has its roots in different focus areas: e-commerce, in store and in warehouse. Some OMS providers, like IBM (Sterling) and OrderDynamics, provide modules as an extension of an ERP system, while players like Manhattan Associates, Kibo, KBRW and Fluent Commerce provide standalone systems. An OMS provides workflow capabilities to manage processes from order capturing, validation and payment authorisation over fraud checking, sourcing and backorder management to pick, pack, ship and transactional order notifications. Return management can also be tackled with an OMS. However, the most important point to emphasise is that the inventory priority and allocation are manageable via the

Fig. 5.14 Seamless omni-channel experiences along channels and touchpoints

sourcing rules. Obviously, each of these OMS solutions has its own strengths and weaknesses, and finding the perfect match calls for an assessment of the individual requirements, such as the total cost of ownership; the degree of automation; the omni-channel scenarios covered out of the box; the scope of channels, geographies and currencies; the support of multiple warehouse locations; API access and interfaces; and the roadmap for further evolution. Furthermore, the potential impact of new network strategies on legacy systems needs to be assessed.

Implementing the Omni-channel
For the basic set-up, different components are essential for integrated omni-channel fulfilment: order orchestration, inventory management, store fulfilment, customer service and integration:

- *Order orchestration* includes the tracking of the order state, intelligent order routing, workflow definitions and notifications, order exceptions, the management of partial shipments, order splitting, drop shipping, recurring

orders, presale and back orders, order versioning, tax calculation, return and fraud management and payment processing.
- *Inventory management* covers stores, drop-ship vendors, distribution centres, in-transit inventory, supply chain visibility and ability to promise (ATP).
- *Store fulfilment* refers to the omni-channel scenarios: ship from store, store pick-up, click and collect, store to store, ship to store and pick and pack.
- *Customer service* refers to the access to order details, order capturing, modification, cancellation and refunds as well as the order escalation workflow.
- *Integration* is essential for the seamless interaction with carriers, stores, merchandising systems and warehouse management.

The journey towards the omni-channel is constructed on four building blocks: planning, inventory visibility, allocation and fulfilment. Everything starts with data. To plan and position inventory efficiently, you need to understand the demand situation based on a data-driven approach, ideally supported by a CDP. In other words, product tracking needs to be enabled on a unique identifier, such as the serial number. Once the unique product identification has been ensured, analytics tools visualise your sales and accurate inventory. You should take influencing events into account, like channel-specific marketing campaigns, to ground your decisions on valid data. Second, inventory visibility is the basis on which to rethink and improve your supply chain network. That visibility supports the usage of individualised assortments at the store level to address the demand more precisely. Third, that goes hand in hand with optimised inventory allocation to ensure, via dynamic sourcing rules, that the customer receives his or her order in the most relevant way. Via sourcing and priority rules, you can define different priority criteria, such as the fastest order route, the most cost-efficient one and the geographically most suitable one. Even expected peaks due to marketing campaigns can be reflected. Based on criteria, the OMS automatically identifies the best fulfilment method to meet the customer demand while securing your profitability target. Finally, based on the planning, inventory visibility and allocation, you can strategically establish smartly positioned shadow inventories. To keep the cost and effort under control, the shadow inventory is often integrated into existing stores and is moved dynamically, triggered by demand.

In return for managing the shadow inventory, extra benefits, like an order priority or exclusive access to selected creations, incentivise the selected stores. An alternative way of incentivising the omni-channel is via the margin. The inventory availability is one asset. The client access is another, but its true value is unlocked when both assets find their match. Therefore, one option is to split the margin between the inventory access of one partner and the client access of another partner. There are multiple options to incentivise customer-centric action, and each brand defines its own rules.

Use Case Example
Looping back to our gentleman in the Munich store, in the meantime, the sales associate has checked the availability of the desired timepiece. He could not find it in either an internal or an external store, but he redirects the customer to the online shop. Based on the brand-owned affiliate programme for employees, linked to the CDP, the sales associate has his own ID acting as a unique identifier when added to shared URLs.

Hence, the sales associate asks the customer: 'May I share with you all the details of the timepiece you are interested in?' Following the customer's confirmation, the sales associate navigates to the relevant reference online in the brand-owned online shop. He adds his affiliate ID to the link and generates, for instance, a QR code for the customer. The sales associate prints this QR code in store on the back of his business card. In a paperless scenario, the QR code is displayed on the in-store device to enable the customer to scan the code directly from the screen. In the next step, the in-store visit is mapped via a unique identifier, like the personal affiliate ID of the sales associate, with an online shop session. As soon as the customer puts the article into the cart and runs the check-out process, the affiliate commission or another incentive is credited to the sales associate.

Thinking further, offering an in-store return option allows another personal interaction between the sales associate and the individual customer. First, the sales associate needs to understand the reason for the return. Accordingly, he or she tries to find an alternative article variance that matches the customer's expectations better. The cycle starts again. The bonding between the sales associate and the individual customer evolves.

In the best case, the service offered surpasses the expected level to make a difference. That becomes obvious from the Kano model, which states that some customer requirements have little or no influence on customer satisfaction.[40] These requirements are also called basic requirements. Brand differentiation via basic requirements, such as a functioning online shop or a seamless fulfilment experience, does not change the game: it goes without saying. So far, we have discussed omni-channel sales scenarios that also involve omni-channel return scenarios. That is essential to act in a customer-centric manner but does not exceed expectations as long as no service personalisation is reflected.

The crux of the matter is that the non-fulfilment of basic requirements leads to dissatisfaction but their fulfilment does not lead to enthusiasm. The decisive factors are the enthusiasm requirements that positively surprise the customer because they were not expected or are fulfilled innovatively. How can brands exceed customers' expectations? How can omni-channel fulfilment be turned into an omni-personal experience? In the next two subchapters, we examine differentiation strategies rooted in product transparency and personalisation.

5.4.1 End-to-End Traceability Delivers the Agility Required to Simplify Supply Chain and Inventory Management

Chopard, in 2013, launched its first Green Carpet Collection made of fairly mined gold from certified mines and precious stones verified by the Responsible Jewellery Council.[41] Tiffany has its own diamond workshops and does not buy from middlemen. In its workshops, a vertically integrated jewellery maker applies laser inscription to track all diamonds larger than 0.18 carats thanks to microscopic codes.[42] Cartier has announced its interest in blockchain technology to trace the origin of precious stones and metals.[43]

François-Henry Bennahmias, CEO at Audemars Piguet, stated in our interview: 'Brands will have to be transparent, with no limitation. They will also have to be more caring than ever.' Where does the creation come from? What is it made of? Who owned it previously? Those questions are not new. In a time when sustainability, social and environmental responsibility, fair labour conditions and transparent supply chains are moving into the customer focus, it is becoming increasingly important to communicate values and responsibilities clearly to your customers. On the one side, it is a matter of transparency and showing responsibility towards customers. On the other side, it is at the centre of ensuring supply chain and inventory visibility to unlock the omni-channel and to leverage profitability based on the principles of circularity.

The objective of end-to-end traceability is to grant each product a digital product identity through a digital twin, NFT or digital passport that holds all the product-related information. Typically, a digital identifier is attached to the product to capture all the information along the value chain—from raw material to finished product and even beyond—enabling a circular economy. When looking at end-to-end traceability, it is important to differentiate between the up- and downstream product life cycle (Fig. 5.15).

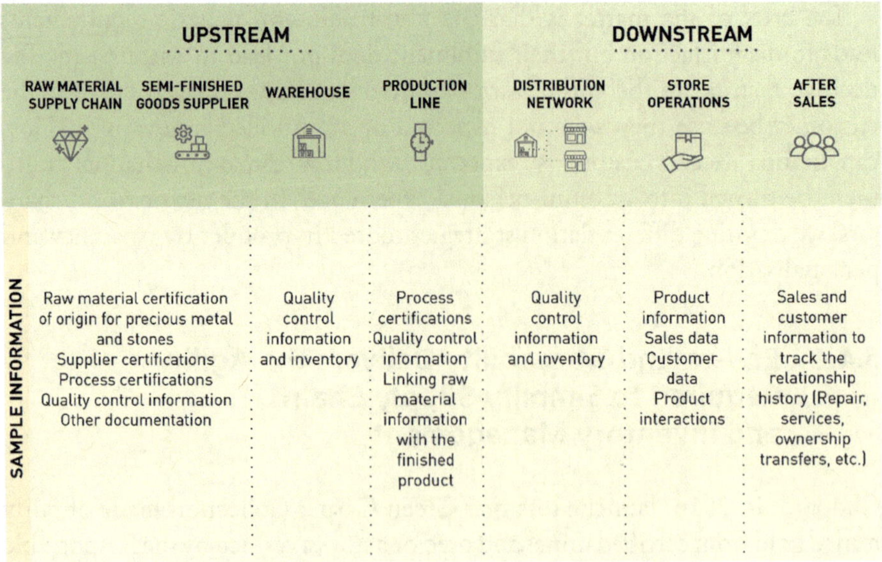

	UPSTREAM				DOWNSTREAM		
RAW MATERIAL SUPPLY CHAIN	SEMI-FINISHED GOODS SUPPLIER	WAREHOUSE	PRODUCTION LINE	DISTRIBUTION NETWORK	STORE OPERATIONS	AFTER SALES
SAMPLE INFORMATION	Raw material certification of origin for precious metal and stones Supplier certifications Process certifications Quality control information Other documentation	Quality control information and inventory	Process certifications Quality control information Linking raw material information with the finished product	Quality control information and inventory	Product information Sales data Customer data Product interactions	Sales and customer information to track the relationship history (Repair, services, ownership transfers, etc.)

Fig. 5.15 End-to-end traceability

The upstream product life cycle covers the process from raw material sourcing, production and manufacturing to the finished creation in the warehouse. The major benefit of traceability in the upstream part is transparency about the product's origin and accurate inventory visibility. Hard luxury players are starting to apply RFID and blockchain in the upstream part. However, their major focus lies on the downstream part as a prerequisite of the omni-channel.

The downstream product life cycle refers to the product distribution within a brand's network via in-store operations and customer engagement to after-sales service and ownership transfer. The advantages of traceability in the downstream part are linked to product authenticity and extended customer services.

In general, for maximum transparency, the transponder or identifier should be attached to the carrier of the value as early as possible in the production process. There are different tracking technologies, such as RFID, NFC, QR codes and barcodes, to trace products, but not all of those technologies work on metal and precious stones, as needed in the jewellery and watch segment. All tracking technologies allow firms to access and update the digital twin of the product with additional information.

RFID, NFC, QR Codes and Barcodes

NFC, QR codes or barcodes are often attached to or printed on separate stickers or cards as they should be visible and scannable. Hence, they need to be paired manually with the reference as they are not a finished product component. Differently, RFID or NFC microchips can be embedded directly into the wrist band or the back of a watch or jewellery creation. Basically, chips are embedded in materials like glass, ceramics or plastics. Direct embedding of the chip in metal is not possible due to the tension coefficient. In consequence, the chip for a timepiece can be planted in the centre of the crystal case covering the dial or back of a watch. With the milestone of this ability to merge product and microchip into one unit, the application possibilities are expanding to the level of smartwatches. The innovative STISS glass, for example—STISS stands for 'Swiss Technology Inside Smart Sapphire'—adds contactless payment functionality to an analogue watch.[44] If we consider this development further, the watch world can ally with exclusive programmes like the American Express Centurion Card to enable VIP customers to pay via their upgraded mechanical smartwatch. It takes little fantasy to imagine how this innovation is inventing a new generation of watches. Brands like Swatch are showing how it works with the 'SwatchPay' programme.

Deep Dive: RFID and NFC

Radio-frequency identification (RFID) devices and their subset NFC (near-field communication) are radio transmission technologies that operate actively, that is, through an external battery power supply, or passively, through electromagnetic inductive power transmission. That is like today's wireless-charging smartphones or ear pods. RFID devices have existed since the end of the Second World War and became smaller and smaller over the years. The original military application moved into industrial and consumer applications, for example credit cards, smartphones, electronic entrance systems and price and tracking tags, as well as watches. The miniaturisation of the latest RFID chip generation is impressive and today is in the range of a square millimetre or even less. Each RFID microchip is equipped with an antenna that is also used to supply power, its main purpose being to read the chip's data via radio frequency within a certain distance at any time. Advanced RFID devices may contain microprocessors, programmable encryption information and various security and encryption methods, such as blockchain technology, to ensure that only authorised users can read the data.

To identify and track materials and products, an RFID microchip can be attached to every single product component. This chip tracks different events, such as the dates of quality control, sell-in, sell-out and return. These data generate numerous insights and accelerate the stocktaking process tremendously. In parallel, the data accuracy benefits from RFID as the stocktaking reaches 99 per cent precision compared with manual stocktaking.[45]

These figures bring us to one of the big questions of tracing technologies: how can their profitability be quantified?[46] For the time being, there is no generic answer to that question. The profitability depends on the individual use case and the company context. In general, a technology like RFID is best integrated at the beginning of the value chain, that is, in the raw material. This makes it possible to achieve maximum success at the end of the chain, such as increased turnover. Within the supply chain and distribution network, this calls for close collaboration and holistic thinking. Therefore, we recommend undertaking an assessment to identify and estimate your cost-saving potential.

For example, the Chinese Jeweller Chow Tai Fook puts the jewellery creations of interest on a smart tray to showcase the creation to the visitor.[47] Each tray is equipped with an RFID tag; likewise, each piece of jewellery has its own RFID tag. In that way, the store has transparency on the viewing history of each creation. It also allows the identification of potential inventory improvements, which is particularly valuable when you are facing limited shelf space in your stores. A/B testing of the best in-store positioning is possible. In the case of Chow Tai Fook, slow-moving products are transferred to another store and are even melted down to be transformed into new creations if the inventory transfer does not trigger sales. These drastic decisions require a clear data foundation, which is ensured through the RFID tags in this case.

Blockchain

When you are looking for data transparency and security, blockchain might be an excellent choice. This technology allows you to merge and store all the data points captured along the value chain transparently and securely. Blockchain is used in a decentralised database by different users, who check the chain's validity from the product origin and any transfers to the last transaction. Whenever a new block element is validated, the blockchain is extended by the new timestamped block and remains accessible to the user network.[48] Thanks to the transparency within the blockchain, the actual owner of a stolen item is in control, being able to flag and share that event with the whole network. If a stolen watch reappears in your brand-controlled internal or external brand store, the sales associate is empowered to identify the legitimate owner. It is self-explanatory that this authentication process detects counterfeits too. In conclusion, blockchain technology grants the ultimate transparency, encoding and decoding a common history between brand and customer. This relationship is easily leveraged for add-on loyalty services. Specialised blockchain providers in the luxury segment are Everledger, Aura, Arianee, WIseKey, Tracr and Adresta.

Deep Dive: Blockchain Specialists Everledger, WIseKey, Tracr and Adresta

Everledger is a technology company focusing on blockchain and intelligent labelling to increase transparency in respect of item origin and ownership. Everledger makes these data available to customers and stakeholders along the value chain, such as producers, manufacturers, certification houses and retailers. In collaboration with Chow Tai Fook and the Gemological Institute of America (GIA), the company launched a digital solution to share diamond grading reports with customers via blockchain.[49]

Aura is a platform aiming to simplify digital security for customers. It grants customers access to a product's history and proof of authenticity.[50] The platform is a consortium of Ethereum blockchain specialist ConsenSys, Microsoft and luxury conglomerate LVMH. The platform targets the entire luxury industry and after first collaborations with Louis Vuitton and Parfums Christian Dior, the Aura Blockchain consortium has been introduced in partnership with LVMH, Richemont and the Prada Group, recently also OTB joined the club.

The Paris-based Arianee project is an independent open-source initiative with the mission to build a global blockchain standard for digital certification in the luxury industry.[51] The watchmakers Breitling and Vacheron Constantin have placed their trust in the decentralised and secure timepiece verification offered by the Arianee protocol to provide an augmented digital identity for their creations.

The Cybersecurity specialist WIseKey offers, under the product name 'WIseAuthentic', a dedicated solution for watchmakers like Hublot, Bulgari and Favre-Leuba.[52] The method combines secure NFC WIseKey NanoSealRT® microchips with cloud-based track-and-trace software to register and authenticate all its timepieces using blockchain technology. In that context, it is important to keep in mind that NFC is mainly used for secure transaction functionality, such as the activation of a watch warranty and anti-counterfeiting (see also Sect. 5.5.4).

Tracr is a diamond industry-focused traceability platform belonging to the diamond market leader De Beers (Fig. 5.16).[53] The platform claims to be 'the first organisation securely tracking a diamond across the diamond value chain—from mine to cutter and polisher through to the jeweller'. You might also be interested to know that Chow Tai Fook is a participant in Tracr's pilot programme.

Finally, the Swiss start-up Adresta creates blockchain-based digital certificates for timepieces.[54] These certificates are stored securely on the Web application together with the history of the watch from manufacturer to service and repair, including pre-owned sales. Adresta is committed to changing the customer experience in the luxury goods industry by creating trust and transparency using new technologies.

The list of providers outlines the variety of options. However, the individual play of single companies is restricted by the lack of scalability and the additional costs linked to that lone-warrior approach. Hence, the creation of a consortium was a fundamental step to set the industry standard in terms of the blockchain protocol applied. That is the basis to unlock scalability.

In addition to the communication transparency gained vis-à-vis the customer, the end-to-end tracking of an item facilitates customer behaviour analysis and, hence, the derivation of new customer-oriented services. It is ultimately the only method to realise the fast and flexible processing of orders, which is indispensable in an omni-channel context.

5.4.2 Last-Mile Management at Scale Is the Philosopher's Stone

Brands invest a considerable amount of money and effort in exclusive marketing, unique product design and elaborate packaging. They keep full control over in-store ceremonies. Last-mile management is the bottleneck for luxury when it comes to online orders and home delivery. On the one hand, Amazon and other companies have set high standards with same-day delivery; on the other hand, luxury brands are often dependent on external delivery providers. Linked to this approach is always a certain risk that the delivery experience will underperform the customer expectation. An even greater risk stems from the fact that the customer will not differentiate between the product and the delivery. For the customer, they count as one experience. The delivery resonates as the latest and therefore most relevant brand impression, also known as the novelty effect. Because of this crucial position within the customer

5 Digital Transformation of the Omni-personal Customer Journey

Fig. 5.16 Ten/ten collection, De Beers Group, 2021 (Printed with De Beers Group permission)

journey, it is even more important to make a convincing impression during the product handover—there is no chance of being left behind when loyalty is risked literally in the last mile.

Luxury brands are addressing this challenge with their own VIP delivery services; external service providers also understand the upmarket demands of the industry. JD's Luxury Express in China offers a white-glove service that delivers orders to the customer's home with an electric vehicle instead of the standard scooter.[55] YNAP, Bulgari, Gucci and Hermès also provide VIP services, like Rolls Royce delivery, handover by a uniformed sales associate with a bodyguard or same-day delivery with a 'you try, we wait' option. The latter assumes that the customer and his preferences are already known, so the selection of creations brought and presented by the personal sales associate is relevant. It is intended for those VIP customers who are willing to order online or by phone but do not want to miss the sales ceremony. In the case of high-end jewellery or timepiece presentations, such a private sales ceremony at the customer's place or in a hotel suite can last for a happy hour, including a glass of champagne or a cup of tea.[56] The experience lacks nothing and offers the utmost discretion. The only downside is that these extra services are only available in metropoles like London or Paris, where the direct proximity to the customer makes them easy to implement with the existing infrastructure.

The described personal last-mile services are certainly a differentiator but are difficult to scale to a broader audience. Nevertheless, we can see some interesting attempts to approach personalised delivery at scale. One is that companies such as YNAP have started to offer local premium delivery options, which allow delivery according to customer-defined delivery windows and evening delivery. Second, this ensures that the customer is available in person at the time of delivery. There are also first pilot projects that make delivery à la 'Lieferando' trackable via an app and allow real-time communication with the delivery person.[57] Both ideas help to ensure a positive delivery experience to satisfy the customer's wish and surpass the expectation.

5.5 Implement the Best After-Sales Service to Attain Enhanced Customer Loyalty

With the democratisation of luxury, the business is scaled but not the after-sales services. Customers, happy to be able to call themselves a customer of brand X at last, have flooded the luxury brands with demand. Luxury could afford a certain degree of ignorance—or at least thought itself secure in this. The potential offered by customer life cycle management remained unexploited. This is now changing.

When one of the authors bought a watch from a Paris-based luxury brand three years ago, the reordering of a bracelet became a special experience. The modular principle of the collection was promoted online: combine the watch freely with different bracelets. This idea promised variety and diversity. The only obstacle was that ordering the interchangeable bracelets was not possible online. This led to the customer visiting an external partner store in Munich.

5 Digital Transformation of the Omni-personal Customer Journey

There, she was told that the collection was not stocked and could not be ordered. The second attempt led to eBay in the hope of finding an authorised online dealer, but only vintage bracelets were offered. Finally, she wrote a request to the official brand customer service. A few days later, she received an answer by e-mail. After the product and price details had been clarified, the customer placed the order and transferred the amount. While all the e-mail communication was in English, the order was confirmed in French—without giving the total value or listing the product references to confirm the order's scope.

That event happened three years ago; today, the story would probably—and hopefully—be different. Nevertheless, it shows that omni-personal communication is based on mutual respect and professionalism across touchpoints. When a brand promotes interchangeable watch straps online, why not offer those in the existing online shop? When an external brand partner is not willing to order the requested strap, who else is? When a brand knows that the customer speaks English, why send a French order confirmation? When a brand fears that there is any doubt about the total value or the references in scope, why not clarify all the order details in the order confirmation? All those moments are potential show stoppers and truly test whether the customer, in spite of everything, still wants to buy—keeping in mind that we are referring to a follow-up purchase.

The story shows that creating enhanced brand loyalty through customer-centric after-sales services is a supreme discipline. Relationship building is unquestionably the greatest challenge and the greatest opportunity at the same time. However, we all know that, without stable relationships and the principle of reciprocity, we would achieve nothing. That is true for Monsieur Cartier and Mademoiselle Chanel, for brands and conglomerates, for you and me. We also know that it costs five times more to gain a new customer than to retain an existing customer.[58]

We will discuss some introductory scenarios in detail in the following sub-chapters. First, your friend is a loyal customer and admirer of Van Cleef & Arpels. For the launch of new collections, she receives personalised invitations to in-store preview events. Second, as a loyal Tiffany customer, you do not need to worry about being spammed with irrelevant marketing e-mails. Your personal sales associate is there for you when it counts. As we described in Sect. 5.2.4, the sales associate even reminds you of your wedding anniversary and remembers your preferences. Third, Bulgari has extended its glamorous brand image to home interior design and luxury hotels to surround the body and soul with brilliant beauty. Anyone staying at one of the Bulgari Hotels will probably share a social media post or two with friends. Last, your uncle loves Breitling watches and installs the official Breitling app to add all his collectables to his digital collection. It makes him happy to receive service reminders via push notification.

5.5.1 In-Store Customer Service Prepares for New Extensions

Beyond sales ceremonies, in-store service is an important stage for after-sales relationship building. This happens via special loyalty treatments like VIP events, extended services—maintenance, repair, return and pick-up services—or innovative experiences. A brand has a responsibility to give customers enough good reasons to visit a store regularly. All these initiatives bestow respect and a feeling of belonging on the individual.

VIP events are a great way to tell VIP customers that they are special. Brands like Boucheron regularly organise exclusive dinner events for VIP customers to enable them to become acquainted with each other personally, discuss the brand's plan for the future and receive direct customer feedback. The secret of these events is to keep the audience small, enabling people to connect on an individual level. Hence, Boucheron invites a maximum of 20 persons.[59] Broadening the audience diminishes the prestige factor. Hence, VIP events alone are not sufficient to reach all loyal customers. Of course, brands schedule collection previews or special offers for a wider audience of brand-loyal persons.

Luxury brands like Louis Vuitton and Ferrari have realised that offering a lifetime warranty for a purchased item enhances customers' trust in the brand. If necessary, they repair items professionally and in a brand-consistent manner. A positive side effect of such a 'maintenance' visit is that the customer has a direct contact point with the sales associate. This means immediate feedback if the customer is not yet 100 per cent satisfied. It also implies situational opportunities to introduce new collections. Jeweller Renésim does not offer a lifelong warranty, but the customer has the right to alter a piece of jewellery for free twice after the purchase.[60]

Over the last years, it has become a strategy of luxury watchmakers like Ulysse Nardin, Breitling, Jaeger-LeCoultre, Cartier, Officine Panerai, IWC Schaffhausen, Rolex and Hublot to offer warranty extensions for up to ten years on top of the standard warranty duration. In return, the brands capture the customers' contact details, like their e-mail address or phone number and marketing consent. This is a fundamental step in entering into dialogue with a customer. Simultaneously, it leads to a query of personal data to qualify for a warranty extension. Depending on the culture and context, brands must take local differences into account to avoid customer discomfort and unwanted stopgap solutions. For example, it makes little sense to ask a Shanghainese customer for his e-mail address. That person potentially uses his mobile phone countless times a day but the e-mail inbox only very rarely. The same logic applies when you ask an 80-year-old man who has neither a mobile phone number nor an e-mail address for one of these. In the worst case, the external partner starts to invent dummy customer data to have the warranty extension granted.

Typically, the customer is asked proactively during the in-store sales ceremony whether he or she wants to benefit from a warranty extension. The same principle is used to offer birthday surprises in exchange for birthday information.

5.5.2 Subscription for Communication, Services and Products Builds Relationships

Constantly talking is not necessarily communicating.
—Charlie Kaufman, American Author

Corresponding to Kaufman's words, one-directional news and nothingness are not communicating in a proper sense. Only dialogue and the relevance of the message to the recipient create resonance. Therefore, it is essential to listen to the customer, understand his or her personal needs and align all communication accordingly.

For personalisation to work well, it is advisable to assign a personal sales associate to each customer. With today's technical possibilities, the principle of the 'same face to the customer' strengthens the relationship between the customer and the brand. CRM and clienteling tools make this possible. Through frequent encounters with the same person, we find them to be increasingly likeable and trustworthy. In psychology, this effect is also known as the mere-exposure effect.[61] We all prefer to read messages from friends and acquaintances rather than calls to action from strangers. We appreciate when people remember us as we do not like telling them our interests repeatedly, as happens in the film *Groundhog Day*.

Chanel's 'Inside Chanel' micro-page and YouTube channel satisfy the brand fans' thirst for knowledge about Coco Chanel.[62] The poetically designed microsite does not impose itself but is found by all those who want to feel connected to the brand—those who want to be notified about every new short video and sign up for the newsletter. The initiative contributes directly to the brand myth. When communication is perceived as inspiring and relevant, people are happy to subscribe to hear from a brand regularly via a newsletter, a sales associate or social media notifications as long as the recipient remains in control of the communication type and frequency.

In the previous chapter, we already mentioned that extended services—another idea beyond the communication and service subscription—make the product variety accessible to the customer. New customer behaviour makes the product subscription business model increasingly interesting. The jewellery subscription service Opulent Box delivers authentic luxury creations from prestigious brands like Chopard and others quarterly.[63] Certificates of authenticity and extra goodies are included in the price of US$25,000 per delivery. All jewellery creations are curated by a personal concierge based on the individual customer's taste.

As another example, we can mention Hermès's Apple smartwatch. With a price of around US$1000, this watch appears to be more affordable than a fine watch from IWC or Omega. However, Apple junkies tend to buy the latest model as soon as it is available—every year—and, within only a few years, they may have spent more than the one-off investment in a fine watch. Which brand do you think had more touchpoints with its customers within the same time frame—Apple or Omega?

5.5.3 Online Reviews and Recommendations Trigger Word of Mouth

Whenever an experience blows people's mind, they are much more likely to express and share their emotions, both positive and also increasingly negative (bashing), with their friends and family, online and offline. It is crucial for people to share their experience because word of mouth has become a cornerstone of e-commerce. It implies that prospective customers search the Web, with all its forums and social media platforms, before purchasing. With Amazon, it has even become natural to find customer reviews directly on product detail pages, and the personalised recommendation system triggers 35 per cent of Amazon's revenue.[64] Clearly, people listen to other people—one of the key principles in marketing. According to a European study by Nielsen, personal recommendations are the most trusted by 78 per cent of respondents, followed by online recommendations with 60 per cent and brand websites with 54 per cent.[65] Hence, it should be normal for brands to invest in a social listening strategy to identify opportunities. By doing so, they also target loyal customers to convert them into brand ambassadors.

5 Digital Transformation of the Omni-personal Customer Journey

In conclusion, brands should proactively encourage customers to share their thoughts. Ways are manifold: starting with a social media campaign and ending with a personalised after-sales e-mail, which, in addition to the Net Promoter Score (NPS), queries the individual brand experience (Fig. 5.17). The NPS of luxury watchmaker Vacheron Constantin asks the customer to rate, on a scale from 1 to 10, how likely they are to recommend the brand to a friend.

In every customer journey, we find three key moments:

- *The zero moment of truth*: when a person forms an initial picture of a brand based on others' reviews of their experiences.
- *The first moment of truth*: when a potential customer physically sees a product for the first time.
- *The second moment of truth*: when the customer actively uses a product. This closes the cycle.

5.5.4 Mobile Apps Are an Engaging Tool to Build a Common History

Mobile applications open up new contact and service opportunities whenever and wherever the user wants them. Once installed, the application makes numerous features available digitally during the customer journey, thus acting as a continuous link between brand and customer.

Fig. 5.17 The Net Promoter Score captures the recommendation likelihood of customers on a scale from 1 to 10 (Image: Olivier Le Moal - stock.adobe.com)

Awareness and Engagement

Digital learning applications are a good starting point to connect with a prospective customer at an early stage. The 'Watch Essentials' mobile app of the Fondation de la Haute Horlogerie (FHH) is an engaging training app for watch enthusiasts who are interested in a 360-degree view of the watchmaking industry.

On the brand level, it makes sense to integrate brand insights and the product catalogue to display product details and enable the creation of a wish list. In addition, gamified try-on experiences and personalised product and event recommendations, including a booking feature, can be leveraged.

The omni-channel can be strengthened by offering location-based services and rewards when the potential customer is close to or entering a store. Push notifications are the instrument of choice to draw the customer's attention to special offers or a shop in the immediate vicinity (see Sect. 5.2.1). Of course, a reason should always be given, indicating why the visit is worthwhile: to see the reference on the wish list in real life, to be surprised or to experience something unique. Visitors can be motivated to scan reference QR codes in store. The accompanying use of the mobile app in the shop leads on average to the customer staying seven minutes longer.[66]

Digital learning in store also simplifies the work and life of sales associates by providing mobile solutions for customer support and questions. Engaging in knowledge sharing packaged in gamified experiences motivates customer-centric thinking. For example, brands impart specific product knowledge in a quiz or give badges and rewards to heavy users who interact continuously with the brand and its products.

Conversion and Fulfilment

In a mobile application, customers expect check-out features or online reservations, as needed for a click-and-collect scenario. In addition, item authenticity plays a major role in luxury. The start-up Entrupy targets the challenge of being sure that the item offered on an online marketplace is the original product and not a counterfeit.[67] Entrupy offers a scalable artificial intelligence mobile application that compares countless product images in no time to control the authenticity of luxury creations and to identify counterfeit goods instantly at the moment of purchase. The company charges around US$10 per authentication process, and it is used first and foremost by reselling marketplaces to benefit from authentication accuracy of 96 per cent. The solution is predominantly applied for handbag checks, but obviously it is transferable to the world of jewellery and watches.

Watch CSA offers a hard luxury authentication service based on deep learning and artificial intelligence. As a user, you upload a picture of the timepiece. The algorithm automatically compares its serial or reference number with images of verified timepieces. In this way, you can identify counterfeits in real time. Successfully verified pieces are granted a certificate.

There is a clear benefit of these digital self-service authenticity checks: they avoid the walk of shame into a physical store where a sales associate potentially tells you that your timepiece is a counterfeited one. Keeping those negative emotions outside your brand temple is an achievement for the customer and the brand.

After Sales and Loyalty

Imagine that you receive a Tank timepiece for your birthday. The sales associate recommends downloading the brand's mobile app on your phone. You register with your contact details and marketing consent. You scan the authenticity certificate or digital watch passport, as already introduced by Breitling or by Vacheron Constantin based on the Arianee protocol for its 'Les Collectionneurs' timepieces (Fig. 5.18).[68] The serial number and thus the timepiece are added to your digital collection. That digital collection is the place where you collect and manage all your treasures—timepieces and jewellery—from a certain brand as well as others. It is your digital jewellery box, consisting of all the creations that you own and dream of (wish list). Moreover, the mobile application represents a smart way to connect with other like-minded brand enthusiasts in a kind of elite community. The success of expert talk on platforms like Clubhouse illustrates this idea.

Various extensions are conceivable. The mobile application of Chrono24 displays the value evolution of timepieces over time. Imagine that the mobile application sends push notifications for special events and battery service reminders or allows you to track the status of requested repairs. The mobile app gives advice on the nearest store physically or virtually and allows the customer to book an appointment with the personal sales associate. Blockchain technology helps to prove and authorise ownership unforgettably and to transfer the reference ownership from one generation to the next.

These ideas provide inspiration for how mobile applications can act as a customer's best friend and supporter along the customer journey. There are five different types of mobile applications:

- *Native application*: This is built for a specific platform, such as iOS or Android, and is downloaded via an app store. A native app runs on the

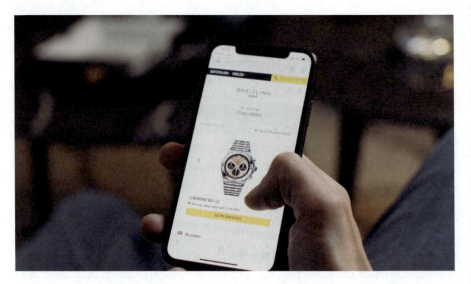

Fig. 5.18 Digital watch passport, Breitling, 2021 (Printed with Breitling's permission)

    device itself and integrates APIs to provide a broad spectrum of features. The application needs to be developed for each operating system separately: for Android in Java and for iOS in Swift or Objective-C.
- *Web application*: This is accessed via the Internet browser and adapts to the device. A Web application does not need to be downloaded and installed because it is not native to a defined system. The spectrum of features is limited, and the usability is affected by data transmission capabilities. Web applications are built in JavaScript, CSS and HTML5.
- *Hybrid application*: This is a combination of a Web and a native application, distributed via native app stores. Its usability is close to the native application experience because the hardware APIs of the smartphone are accessible via the geolocation camera and so on, without being native to a certain system. The disadvantages are that it does not work offline, and the more complex the application, the slower the loading times as the app acts with the intermediate layer of the Web browser. Hybrid applications are developed in JavaScripts, CSS and HTML5.
- *Progressive (Web) application*: This is a Web-based application developed by Google and runs in the browser without the need for any installation. It loads quickly and works offline thanks to the application cache feature in modern browsers. Like a Web application, progressive applications are coded in JavaScript, CSS and HTML5.

- *Cross-platform application*: This is similar to a hybrid application as it builds on one code base with a native look and feel on any platform. This is due to the fact that hybrid applications leverage the APIs of the operating system, allowing a substantial part of the source code to be shared between the different platforms without a lack of performance.

Mobile applications facilitate personalised communication, allow targeted push notifications and enhance the brand experience. Likewise, intensive app use is linked to higher sales. However, approximately the same budget is required for publicising an app as for developing it because the investment only pays off when the application is installed and used. We have provided various application examples in this chapter. At the same time, the sense and benefit of the solution should be clear to the customer. Usability should not be sacrificed for tool complexity.

5.6 KPI Tracking and Measurement Is the Basis for Improvement

If you cannot measure it, you cannot improve it.
—Lord Kelvin, British Physicist

It is not about having as much data as possible (big data) but about having enough smart data to make it possible to derive valuable insights. The more precisely you capture and track behavioural information with analytic tools, the more appropriately you can react to your customer's needs and ensure personal relevance in your relationship. The more you listen to the customer, the more details you can recall afterwards to deepen your one-to-one relationships in an iterative process. Or in the words of François-Henry Bennahmias, CEO at Audemars Piguet: 'Data is key, but analysis is even more important'.

It matters to track and learn in real time about a person interested in a brand and its products across touchpoints and channels—offline and online. That builds the data foundation for a 360-degree view of the customer. On the basis of those data, customer signals are interpreted, and assumptions and decisions are made about the right experience to offer for the blueprint. The experience is designed and tested. Thanks again to analytics, the test results generate insights into how to improve and scale the experience to make it more relevant to the customer. This is the main purpose of analytics, which is to understand the actual and control development towards the target in a recurrent loop (Fig. 5.19).

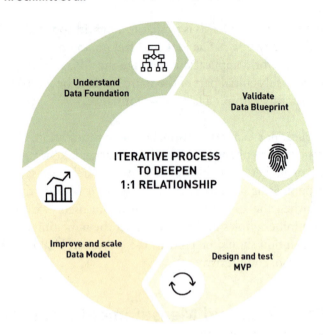

Fig. 5.19 Iterative process to deepen one-to-one relationships

The first condition to make data comparable in an omni-channel world is to harmonise KPIs across online and offline channels along the customer journey. For example, your captured online views of your digital brand advertising correspond to the captured window views of pedestrians passing a physical store. The actual visits generated for your on- or offline brand presence allow you to derive the brand's attraction rate. To achieve this, you put views and visits into their percentage ratio. That rate tells you how appealing and promising the audience perceives your brand presence to be. It is a simple logic that the geographical location of a physical store and the most appropriate attribution model for your digital advertising have a direct impact on brand perception. In other words, you are unlikely to find a Bulgari shop on the same street as a discount shop; it is appropriate to optimise the targeting of online advertising continuously. No jeweller wants to be listed next to an educational page about blood diamonds, even though both pages deal with diamonds.

Second, the harmonised KPIs enable a holistic view that is the key to achieving actionable insights in an omni-channel world. On the one hand, the customer experience benefits from the fact that business potentials are identified faster. On the other hand, costs are controlled better and revenues are increased through data- and performance-driven sales network optimisation.

5 Digital Transformation of the Omni-personal Customer Journey

AWARENESS	ENGAGEMENT	PURCHASE	FULFILLMENT	LOYALTY
On-/Offline Views	Recurrent Visits	Leads	Net Promoter Score (NPS)	Reviews/Referrals
On-/Offline Visits	(Product) Search/ Interaction Rate	Conversion Rate	Customer Satisfaction Rate	Repurchase Rate
Session Duration	(Product) Views per Visitor	Order Value and Items Sold	Customer Service Requests	Purchase Frequency
Cost per Visit	Cost per Interaction	Cost per Lead/ Conversion	Cost per Fulfillment	Cost per Loyalty
Cost per Name	Cost per Name	Cost per Name	Cost per Service	Customer Lifetime Value (CLV)
Cost per Client Preference	Cost per Client Preference	Cost per Client Preference	Cost per Client Preference	Cost per Customer
Subscription Rate	Wishlist Creation Rate	Purchase Cancellation Rate	Return Rate	Newsletter Opening Rate

Fig. 5.20 Illustrative set of common on-site and in-store KPIs along the customer journey

The set of relevant KPIs depends on the company and its objectives. Therefore, this book provides visualisation of an illustrative set of KPIs (Fig. 5.20).

The listed KPIs are relevant in the on-site and in-store context. From an omni-personal standpoint, CRM and clientele-related data, such as a customer's name and his or her preferences, lead to the ultimate objective to learn more about the customer. That starts with the essential account creation and the desired marketing consent to be allowed to enter into a dialogue with the customer as a brand.

Online Data Capturing

Online data capturing allows full transparency from the first user view up to the product review. A key requirement for data capturing is a proper tracking set-up across channels. This refers to the consistent positioning of tracking snippets not only on site but also off site from SEA, SEO, social media networks and referrals to e-mail, the mobile application and even QR codes to be scanned from a classical magazine. In the case of the market leader, Google Analytics, the tracking snippets are based on so-called Urchin Tracking Module (UTM) parameters. Unfortunately, a poor or incomplete tracking set-up leads to wrong conclusions and decisions in product development as well as in marketing. That is why the correct tracking set-up to unlock real-time data exchange and support cross-device traceability acts as the foundation for online analytics.

Tools like Google Analytics, Adobe Online SiteCatalyst and the open-source platform Matomo provide Web-tracking solutions that include user-friendly dashboards that depict KPIs at a glance. Beyond the analysis of raw and aggregated data, click stream and conversion path analysis clarifies the entry and exit points in the customer journey and helps to define objectives and link a monetary value to each achieved objective signal.

Once essential key moments in the conversion path have been identified, companies should use optimisation to keep the user on the site. The A/B test is a particularly useful tool to measure and compare the impact of a new call to action with the bounce rate, session duration and conversion rate. Nevertheless, A/B testing is a quantitative optimisation method. It needs significant traffic rates to generate reliable results. This is often the bottleneck and implies that A/B testing is mainly recommended for frequently visited pages with a clear and comparable KPI set-up. Moreover, the involvement of users and customers in A/B testing or regular walk-the-store sessions is not yet a common practice in luxury—these should have an equal position to mystery shopping, typically carried out by employees or consultants. The benefit of real customer feedback is the fact that customers bring a refreshing perspective to a brand that long-serving employees replace with experience and knowledge over time. However, as a brand, you want to learn from manifold perceptions, including A/B testing.

In general, performance monitoring with an omni-channel tracking tool opens the door to continuous fine-tuning of a brand's marketing attribution model. Based on tracking snippets, defined objectives and active integration with an advertising platform, like the Google Marketing Platform, you can control the marketing ROI of different attribution channels and derive the best budget allocation for your business.

In-Store Data Capturing
In-store data capturing started with the manual counting of people entering a store. That method is inexpensive and applicable by the store staff, but it also gives only a very limited range of information, such as the number of persons, their estimated age and their gender. The data accuracy depends on human eyes. The information precision and completeness risk suffering in peak traffic times, and the data retrieved through observation require manual mapping with the sell-out declaration and CRM database. This mapping is only

5 Digital Transformation of the Omni-personal Customer Journey

possible in cases in which the essential unique identifier is known. Without the mapping between in-store traffic and customer information, the data are still valuable for understanding the store's performance. However, the understanding is limited to store entrance and check-out data. The brand and product interactions between them remain blind spots (Fig. 5.21). The data bring no added value to the customer in an omni-personal sense.

That is why we see the automation of in-store traffic capturing as an investment in relationship building. The link is not obvious at first glance and requires further explanation. Remember Sect. 5.2.1, in which we discussed iBeacons as a positioning technology for devices in store or nearby. Now, we assume that the loyal customer has installed the brand's mobile application. As he or she comes closer to the store, signals are sent to the user's device, and in-store product interaction is tracked in real time on an individual level. That unique recognition of the customer is an asset that plays a vital role in personal relationship building between the sales associate and the customer. The brand and product interaction becomes visible, and the blind spots disappear.

Obviously, this approach does not work for prospective customers who have not yet shared their personal data and consent with a store or brand via a mobile app installation or a traditional client loyalty card. There are alternatives on the market, such as the following:

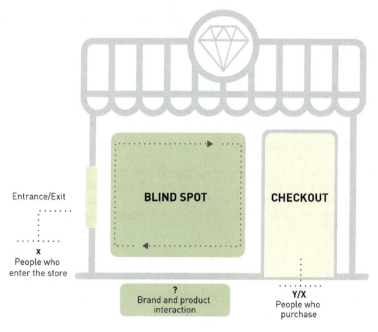

Fig. 5.21 Unlocking the potential of in-store customer monitoring

- *Video cameras* can be installed in store to monitor customer behaviour. Enriched by AI and beyond pure movement tracking, a visitor's attire style, age and gender can be identified. Due to privacy policy regulations, it is important to obtain legal advice regarding this solution. In countries like China, facial recognition is already a common practice, but in the rest of the world, this technology has been viewed with a critical eye, calling for anonymised data. Nevertheless, the immediate recognition of the customer upon entering the shop naturally offers greater scope for service personalisation than the recognition of the customer at the check-out.
- *Radio-frequency or laser sensors* provide a wireless and GDPR-compliant solution to track real-time customer behaviour. In this solution, no pictures are taken. This technology allows one to identify the dimensions of moving objects in a room. In addition, outdoor application of the lasers is possible as long as the sensibility to sunlight is considered. Relevant providers are Sensalytics, Hitachi 3D-Lidar, LASE PeCo and BEA sensors.
- *Wi-Fi trackers* unlock data tracking through in-store Wi-Fi access points. Every mobile device with activated Wi-Fi is identifiable through its search signal for a Wi-Fi hotspot. That signal includes the unique media access control (MAC) address of the mobile device. Interesting providers are Purple, Blix, Walkbase and Bloom Intelligence.

In an end-to-end in-store monitoring approach, it is possible to merge the in-store customer behaviour information with product and sales data in real time, particularly if you combine in-store traffic counting with RFID-based product tracking. That allows conclusions about the effectiveness of the store concept, staff performance, marketing campaigns, product assortment and product presentation, such as the best product position. In their book *Luxury Retail and Digital Management*, Chevalier and Gutsatz refer to an insightful study, outlining the following:

> A product displayed on the end of the aisle sells four to five times more than when it is on a shelf. These presentations are therefore more effective for fast-selling shelf products than for others. However, products that are slow selling will attract more new customers than if they are on the shelves and thus help to increase their market share.[69]

With your own in-store tracking capability, you can derive and define new assumptions and prove them in your daily business. End-to-end monitoring is scalable and nurtures your databases with the data required to extend the descriptive analytics of today towards predictive analytics. This includes using strategies like machine learning or artificial intelligence to forecast future outcomes and their likelihood.

The Oxygen of the Omni-personal

Data analytics alone provides enough material to write books, and we have only one chapter to give a high-level overview. On-site and in-store locations are sales channels, but beyond that we see them increasingly as data collection hubs to manage sales more efficiently. In this chapter, we have considered on-site and in-store data. Both belong to the category of internal data. However, it makes sense to extend that internal view through the integration of external data sources. Finally, it is important to keep a clear and SMART objective in mind and to know at all times what data are needed and why. Probably the know-how is trickiest for companies because it requires a clear understanding of the technologies available on the market, the data aggregation methodology and the visualisation of data in an intuitive and easily understandable way.

If you are looking for a truly customer-centred omni-channel data hub to deal with a complex data landscape, a customer data platform (CDP) helps you to structure and aggregate data and derive the insights that you need. A CDP is a marketing or sales controlled platform that builds on an integrated customer database to collect, unify and expose in real time customer data from online and offline channels to execution systems like marketing or OMS tools. Adobe, Google, Microsoft, Oracle and Salesforce—to mention just the large enterprise vendors—provide CDP solutions besides many smaller players in the highly fragmented market of CDPs.

Certain CDPs orchestrate customer journeys and predictive data modelling, bringing additional intelligence to connected systems, for instance an OMS. Predictive algorithms are at the core of managing the distribution and supply chain more smartly and efficiently to have the inventory exactly where and when the customer demands it—potentially even before the customer is aware of it. In a marketing context, a CDP allows the communication of personalised messages to an individual, considering the full customer journey.

Obviously, some CDP features are known from data lakes, master data management (MDM), data management platforms (DMPs) and CRM systems. However, a CDP represents the next logical step in that evolution, merging different tools like a data lake, DMP or CRM into one consolidated platform.

Different from CDPs, data lakes and MDM are usually enterprise-wide projects, targeting IT and analytics experts and not marketing and end-client-facing teams. Furthermore, data lakes and MDM provide raw data format access only, without real-time updates or the possibility to leverage a cross-channel customer view, as needed for the golden record. In conclusion, with a data lake or MDM, you cannot master customer omni-channel data in real time.

Comparable with a DMP, a CDP is primarily owned by marketing or sales and allows real-time data access. Still, a CDP focuses on known customers with a unique identifier and individual information, while a DMP is dedicated to anonymous user profiles, mainly online data. Via browser cookies, prospective online customers are mapped to certain attributes, like interests or demographics. Via these cookies, the online distribution and display of advertising can be controlled without the need for individual identification of the user.

Finally, you might ask how CRM and CDP differ from each other. CRM systems are primarily used to capture data during direct customer interaction. The data mapping and merging are based on a unique single identifier. In contrast, CDP systems aim to give a holistic 360-degree view of a specific customer by combining all the data that an organisation has about the customer into a unified profile, the golden record. CDPs are designed for dealing with big data volumes from various sources and systems in real time. Moreover, CDPs allow the merging of data by matching multiple identifiers.

In an omni-channel and omni-personal strategy, data analytics is like the oxygen in your lungs. All of your decisions are based on data. All of your measurable results have a reason and an origin. The omni-personal has its roots in conscious decision making. As Edward Deming brilliantly noted: 'Without data, you are just another person with an opinion'.

Notes

1. Reichheld F (2006) The ultimate question: driving good profits and true growth. Harvard Business School Press, Brighton; Reichheld F (1996) The loyalty effect: the hidden force behind growth, profits, and lasting value. Harvard Business School Press, Brighton.
2. Hubbard L (2019) Tiffany & Co. just opened their first men's pop-up shop in NYC. https://www.townandcountrymag.com/style/jewelry-and-watches/a30153239/tiffany-mens-pop-up-shop-2019/. Accessed 6 December 2020.
3. Assum A, Hemmerle M (2018) Multichannel-Strategie als Erfolgsfaktor für eine Luxusmarke. In: Böckenholt I, Mehn A (eds) Konzepte und Strategien für Omnichannel-Exzellenz: Innovatives Retail-Marketing mit mehrdimensionalen Vertriebs- und Kommunikationskanälen. Springer, Wiesbaden, Locations 3576–3858.
4. Rudeloff C, Müller N (2018) Virtual Reality in der Markenkommunikation am Point of Sale—Ergebnisse einer qualitativen Befragung. In: Pietzcker D, Vaih-Baur C (eds) Luxus als Distinktionsstrategie: Kommunikation in der

internationalen Luxus- und Fashionindustrie. Springer, Wiesbaden, pp 301–316.
5. Mackevision (2019) Company website. https://www.mackevision.com/de/referenzen/oris/. Accessed 31 December 2020.
6. Riley D (2018) Gucci employs CR and AR experiences for spring campaign. https://thecurrentdaily.com/2018/03/01/gucci-spring2018-vr-ar-campaign/. Accessed 1 March 2020.
7. Nanda MC (2021) Gucci is selling $12 (virtual) sneakers. https://www.businessoffashion.com/articles/technology/gucci-is-selling-12-virtual-sneakers. Accessed 16 March 2020.
8. WiseKey (2021) WISeKey $WKEY to auction the first ever secure luxury non-fungible token #nft watch on March 31, 2021. https://www.wisekey.com/press/wisekey-wkey-to-auction-the-first-ever-secure-luxury-non-fungible-token-nft-watch-on-march-31-2021/. Accessed 26 March.
9. Baxter N (2019) 7 ways fashion brands are harnessing hologram technology. https://thecurrentdaily.com/2019/10/01/7-ways-fashion-brands-are-harnessing-hologram-technology/. Accessed 1 October 2020.
10. Jiayun K (2020) Holographic installation puts jewelry in the picture. https://www.shine.cn/biz/event/2011079313/. Accessed 7 November 2020.
11. Batat W (2019) The new luxury experience: creating the ultimate customer experience. Springer, Wiesbaden, Location 3188.
12. Webber J (2018) Luxury Consumption, Seen under a Contemporary Light. In: Pietzcker D, Vaih-Baur C (eds) Luxus als Distinktionsstrategie: Kommunikation in der internationalen Luxus- und Fashionindustrie. Springer, Wiesbaden, pp 83–94, p 182, p 174.
13. Batat W (2019) Digital luxury. Sage Publications, Los Angeles, p 177.
14. Journal Du Luxe (2020) Louis Vuitton: un mobile store dans une caravane. https://journalduluxe.fr/louis-vuitton-mobile-store-us/. Accessed 30 November 2020.
15. Luxury Daily (2018) Tiffany launches Paper Flowers in China via Tmall pop-up. https://www.luxurydaily.com/tiffany-launches-paper-flowers-in-china-via-tmall-pop-up/. Accessed 16 August 2020.
16. British Museum (2020) How to explore the British Museum from home. https://blog.britishmuseum.org/how-to-explore-the-british-museum-from-home/. Accessed 27 March 2020.
17. Whiddington R (2021) Show me the Monet: MFA Boston debuts livestreaming on Kuaishou. https://jingculturecommerce.com/mfa-boston-kuaishou-international-museum-day-livestream/. Accessed 6 June 2021.
18. Zhiwei F, Caixiong Z (2021) Changsha subway digital art museum becomes new top destination. http://www.chinadaily.com.cn/a/202104/30/WS608b75f8a31024ad0babb87e.html. Accessed 6 June 2021.

19. Bezamat B (2018) Hermès launches mobile game as part of year-long celebration of play. https://thecurrentdaily.com/2018/03/28/hermes-mobile-game-play/. Accessed 28 March 2020.
20. Phelps N (2021) The Metaverse's first runway show is here—Watch Collina Strada, Bruce Glen, My Mum Made It, and Mowalola's IMVU Debut. https://www.vogue.com/article/imvu-virtual-fashion-show-announcement. Accessed 5 June 2021.
21. Williams Gemma A. (2021) Will Gucci's Digital Bag Disrupt Luxury? https://jingdaily.com/gucci-roblox-dionysus-digital-fashion/. Accessed 31 May 2021.
22. Google Trends (2021) 'Engagement ring' versus 'Cartier ring' in the last 12 months. https://trends.google.de/trends/explore?q=engagement%20ring,cartier%20ring. Accessed 14 March 2021.
23. Spreer P (2018) PsyConversion: 101 Behavior Patterns für eine bessere User Experience und höhere Conversion—Rate im E-Commerce. Springer, Wiesbaden, p 208.
24. Guiltbault L (2020) Jewellery spending is down. It's still a good bet. https://www.voguebusiness.com/companies/jewellery-spending-is-down-its-still-a-good-bet. Accessed 3 July 2020.
25. Binkley C (2021) Private broadcasts are luxury brands' new secret weapon. https://www.voguebusiness.com/companies/private-broadcasts-are-luxury-brands-new-secret-weapon. Accessed 17 March 2021.
26. Accenture (2021) Virtual showcase by Accenture. https://www.youtube.com/watch?v=JZPcSg-9Swc. Accessed 18 March 2021.
27. Jiayun K (2020) Holographic installation puts jewelry in the picture. https://www.shine.cn/biz/event/2011079313/. Accessed 7 November 2020.
28. Daugherty P, Wilson H (2018) Human + machine: reimagining work in the age of AI. Harvard Business Review, Boston.
29. Sigmund R, Thomas-Dingemann T (2018) Die Bedeutung des Lieferanten für den Erfolg des Omnichannel-Händler am Beispiel des selektiven Kosmetikmarktes in Deutschland. In: Böckenholt I, Mehn A (eds) Konzepte und Strategien für Omnichannel-Exzellenz: Innovatives Retail-Marketing mit mehrdimensionalen Vertriebs- und Kommunikationskanälen. Springer, Wiesbaden, Locations 3143–3575.
30. Chaumet (2021) Company homepage. https://inimitablejosephine.chaumet.com/en/. Accessed 28 March 2021.
31. Nason S, Salvacruz J (2017) Case study: competing against bling. Harvard Business Review. May–June:155–159.
32. Aminoff J (2016) Social selling luxury: increase sales by engaging in the digital world. Luxury Sales Academy.
33. Chang A, Mauron P (2020) JingDigital and Digital Luxury Group—WeChat luxury index 2020. JingDigital. https://www.jingdigital.com/en/articles/8255/, p 74. Accessed 3 April 2021.

34. Srun F (2017) Luxury selling: lessons from the world of luxury in selling high quality goods and services to high value clients. Palgrave Macmillan, Hampshire, Locations 1855, 2588.
35. Hapticmedia (2020) Configure your watch in 3D. https://hapticmedia.fr/en/clients-projects/3d-configurator-watch-baume/. Accessed 21 December 2020.
36. Husemann-Kopetzky M (2018) Handbook on the psychology of pricing: 100+ effects on persuasion and influence every entrepreneur, marketer and pricing manager needs to know. Pricing School Press, p 196.
37. Batat W (2019) Digital luxury. Sage Publications, Los Angeles, p 180.
38. Batat W (2019) Digital luxury. Sage Publications, Los Angeles, p 176.
39. EOS (2012) Glänzende Aussichten mit additiver Fertigung von Gold. https://www.eos.info/01_parts-and-applications/case_studies_applications_parts/_case_studies_pdf/de_cases/cs_m_cookson_gold_cpm.pdf. Accessed 1 November 2021.
40. Kreutzer R (2018) Customer Experience Management—wie man Kunden begeistern kann. In: Rusnjak A, Schallmo R (eds) Customer Experience im Zeitalter des Kunden: Best Practices, Lessons Learned und Forschungsergebnisse. Springer, Wiesbaden, pp 193–241.
41. Cappellieri A, Tenuta L (2020) Jewellery between product and experience: luxury in the twenty-first century. In: Gardetti MÁ, Coste-Manière I (eds) Sustainable luxury and craftsmanship: environmental footprints and eco-design of products and processes. Springer Nature Singapore Pte Ltd, Singapore, pp 1–23.
42. Cumenal F (2017) How I did it: Tiffany's CEO on creating a sustainable supply chain. Harvard Business Review. March–April:41–46.
43. Corder R. (2018) Swiss watchmaker tracks timepieces for life using blockchain technology. https://www.watchpro.com/swiss-watchmaker-tracks-timepieces-for-life-using-blockchain-technology/. Accessed 24 September 2020.
44. GQ (2020) Rolex der Zukunft? Technischer Durchbruch könnte aus Luxusuhren eine Smartwatch machen. https://www.gq-magazin.de/mode/artikel/rolex-der-zukunft-technischer-durchbruch-macht-luxusuhren-zu-smartwatch. Accessed 5 August 2020.
45. Jahn M (2017) Industrie 4.0 konkret: Ein Wegweiser in die Praxis. Springer, Wiesbaden, Location 370.
46. Jahn M (2017) Industrie 4.0 konkret: Ein Wegweiser in die Praxis. Springer, Wiesbaden, Location 169.
47. Zhang W, Chen J (2020) Digging for gold with data analytics at Chow Tai Fook. https://store.hbr.org/product/digging-for-gold-with-data-analytics-at-chow-tai-fook/HK1211. Accessed 3 April 2021.
48. Batat W (2019) Digital luxury. Sage Publications, Los Angeles, p 131.
49. Everledger (2020) Company website. https://www.everledger.io/case-study/everledger-with-gia-and-chow-tai-fook/. Accessed 27 December 2020.

50. ConsenSys (2019) LVMH, ConsenSys, and Microsoft announce consortium for luxury industry. https://consensys.net/blog/press-release/lvmh-microsoft-consensys-announce-aura-to-power-luxury-industry/. Accessed 16 May 2020.
51. Arianee (2021) Company website. https://www.arianee.org. Accessed 28 February 2021.
52. WIseKey (2020) Company website. https://www.wisekey.com/solutions/brand-protection/authentic-customer-engagement/. Accessed 27 December 2020.
53. Tracr (2020) Company website. https://www.tracr.com. Accessed 31 December 2020.
54. Adresta (2020) Company website. https://adresta.ch/en. Accessed 31 December 2020.
55. Santhiram S (2020) How luxury brands can leverage e-commerce to bounce back post-COVID-19. https://www.luxurysociety.com/en/articles/2020/04/how-can-luxury-brands-their-e-commerce-game-post-covid19/. Accessed 27 April 2020.
56. Guiltbault L (2020) Jewellery spending is down. It's still a good bet. https://www.voguebusiness.com/companies/jewellery-spending-is-down-its-still-a-good-bet. Accessed 3 July 2020.
57. Heinemann, G (eds) (2019) Der neue Online Handel. Springer, Wiesbaden, p 379.
58. Morgan B (2019) The customer of the future: 10 guiding principles for winning tomorrow's business. Harper Collins, New York, p 176.
59. Kramer L (2010) The globe: how French innovators are putting the "social" back in social networking. Harvard Business Review. October:1–3.
60. Assum A, Hemmerle M (2018) Multichannel-Strategie als Erfolgsfaktor für eine Luxusmarke. In: Böckenholt I, Mehn A (eds) Konzepte und Strategien für Omnichannel-Exzellenz: Innovatives Retail-Marketing mit mehrdimensionalen Vertriebs- und Kommunikationskanälen. Springer, Wiesbaden, Locations 3576–3858.
61. Spreer P (2018) PsyConversion: 101 Behavior Patterns für eine bessere User Experience und höhere Conversion -Rate im E-Commerce. Springer, Wiesbaden, p 255.
62. Inside Chanel (2020) Company website. https://inside.chanel.com. Accessed 31 December 2020.
63. Opulent (2020) Company website. https://www.opulentjewelers.com/opulent-box. Accessed 29 December 2020.
64. Morgan B (2019) The customer of the future: 10 guiding principles for winning tomorrow's business. Harper Collins, New York, p 27.
65. Kreutzer R (2018), Holistische Markenführung im digitalen Zeitalter—Voraussetzung zur Erreichung einer Omnichannel-Exzellenz. In: Böckenholt I, Mehn A (eds) Konzepte und Strategien für Omnichannel-Exzellenz:

Innovatives Retail-Marketing mit mehrdimensionalen Vertriebs- und Kommunikationskanälen. Springer, Wiesbaden, Locations 2366–3140.
66. Heinemann G (eds) (2019) Der neue Online Handel. Springer, Wiesbaden, p 482.
67. Entrupy (2020) Company website. https://www.entrupy.com. Accessed 31 December 2020.
68. Breitling (2020) Company website. https://www.breitling.com/de-de/service/blockchain/. Accessed 31 December 2020; Vacheron Constantin (2020) Company website. https://www.vacheron-constantin.com/en2/services/impeccable-service/authenticity-certificate.html. Accessed 31 December 2020.
69. Chevalier M, Gutsatz M (eds) (2019) Luxury retail and digital management. Wiley, New Jersey, Location 3636.

6

How to Go Omni-personal

Key Aspects

- The omni-personal strategy needs to be embedded in the business unit strategy.
- The owner of the omni-personal strategy has to be chosen from among the Chief Marketing, Sales, Digital, Technology and Chief Information Officer.
- An organisation must have the technical, cultural and human capacity to implement the objectives set within the omni-personal strategy. This requires alignment and implies a fundamental transformation.
- Three emerging approaches are currently available to kick off the omni-personal transformation: the vertically integrated approach, modular marketplaces and e-retail platforms, and the full-stack ecosystem.
- The approach is selected on the brand level based on the intended brand reach and control.

The lack of brand empathy in the customer journey is today's major weakness of omni-channel implementations. While the omni-channel acts as the first step towards the customer, the omni-personal approach is the future. Personalisation must appear neither intrusive nor creepy. The omni-personal model is about empathy, respect, dialogue and relationships. It is about the right word at the right moment and empathy in an increasingly anonymous world.

Becoming omni-personal requires a fundamental transformation of a company's operating model. For many luxury companies today, that represents equally a great challenge and a great opportunity. Besides a cultural shift towards data-driven management, it calls for true collaboration between the different business functions—operations, finance, HR, IT, sales and marketing.

The magic question is how to make that dream come true. The omni-personal transformation starts with strategy. This chapter focuses on the business unit strategy for brands and not on the corporate strategy at the level above.

6.1 The Omni-personal Transformation Starts with Strategy

As illustrated, the business unit strategy needs four key elements (Fig. 6.1):

- *Objectives*: Objectives need to be Specific, Measurable, Achievable, Realistic and Timely (SMART). They refer to numerical values and percentages and define what should be achieved.
- *Target segments*: Target segments define where a business needs to be active and where not. That includes the market focus in a geographic as well as a category sense, for example a focus on jewellery.
- *Competitive advantages*: Competitive advantages answer the question of how to win against the competition. These relate to the brand positioning

Fig. 6.1 The key elements of a business unit strategy

within the value chain and set vertical or horizontal integration priorities. Besides, the distribution network strategy defining the distribution mix across channels creates differentiation.
- *Initiatives*: Initiatives are the list of required projects and actions needed to progress from the current to the target state. They concern the tasks to be performed, which are, for instance, portfolio optimisation to identify profitable merger and acquisition targets or sales opportunities for underperforming brand business divisions.

The brand leadership ensures that the target segments, competitive advantages and initiatives are aligned with the company objectives.

6.2 The Omni-personal Needs to Be Embedded in the Business Unit Strategy

The omni-personal strategy needs to be embedded in the business unit strategy. There, it is divided into four building blocks defined in the business unit strategy from an omni-personal point of view (Fig. 6.2). The omni-personal strategy owner has to be chosen from among the Chief Marketing, Sales, Digital, Technology and Chief Information Officer. It is important that the

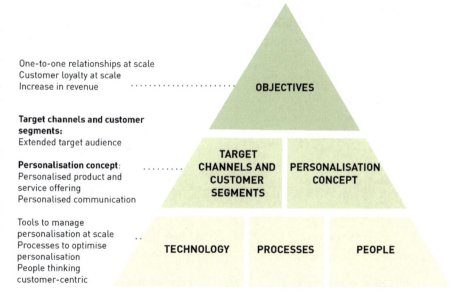

Fig. 6.2 The omni-personal strategy

omni-personal strategy is owned by one executive, although a number of executives might give input or have to agree.

By nature, a business unit strategy should cover a chapter of a business's development and is therefore multi-year by default. While strengthening the omni-personal might be a key aspect of the business unit strategy, the details of the omni-personal strategy might require frequent adjustments due to evolving customer expectations, competitor moves and newly available technologies.

The omni-personal and business unit strategies influence and update each other in an iterative cycle (Fig. 6.3). This mainly concerns the second level, which contains the target channels and customer segments and the personalisation concept. However, these in turn radiate to the first and third levels and can result in the need to make objective corrections or adjustments to the initiatives.

Objectives
The objectives of the omni-personal strategy need to follow the SMART principle. Generally speaking, scalable one-to-one relationship management sustainably increases customer loyalty. This, in turn, leads to an increasing turnover and a decreasing percentage of acquisition costs. In a nutshell it stands for: more relevance, more relationship, more revenue.

Target Channels and Customer Segments
The omni-personal strategy unlocks personalisation at scale, which was exclusively reserved for VIP customers in the past. The interpretation of luxury is

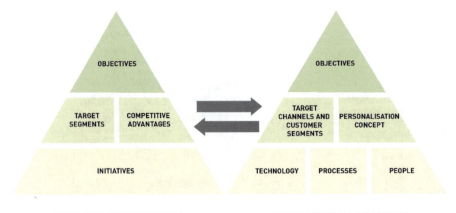

Fig. 6.3 The omni-personal and business unit strategies affect each other

subject to an ongoing transformation process, led by individual dreams and ideas. The new omni-personal potential allows brands to extend their target audience to younger and more global and digital-oriented generations. At the same time, a wider reach pays off positively for a brand's revenue objective.

Personalisation Concept

The personalisation concept builds on products, services and communication. Regarding the product and service, the customer, as an influencer, acts as a co-designer and innovator thanks to social media involvement. When it comes to product configuration, the customer transforms into a co-creator. The customisation of the product by the customer through internet technology at different stages of the value chain requires a vertical structure. In terms of communication, the customer determines when to receive which communication format, how regularly and via which channel. The customer-centric approach puts the customer at eye level with the brand to facilitate fruitful relationships. Of course, the brand remains in control of the customer clustering to define the level of personalisation unlocked for different customer segments.

Initiatives: Technology, Processes, People

An organisation must have the technical, cultural and human capacity to implement the objectives set. Initiatives in the fields of technology, processes and people will be the subject of the following subchapters. They are critical to the success of the business model transformation:

- *Technology* builds the toolbox for key activities like customer relationship management (CRM) or analytics.
- *Processes* enable seamlessness thanks to clear governance flows and structures.
- *People* with the right skills and expertise drive progress and change.

Beyond the business model transformation, common to these three fields is that continuous innovation should have a permanent place in the organisation, enabling it to review and optimise the existing strategies regularly. This allows for a certain degree of flexibility and agility to respond appropriately and promptly to market changes. It makes sense for a dedicated innovation officer or team to shoulder this responsibility. Innovation is indeed the only way to surprise customers positively and to exceed their expectations.

6.2.1 Technology Provides Tools for Omni-personal Experiences

Luxury brands don't need to be early adopters of technology, but luxury brands are early adopters of culture.
 —Ian Rogers, Former Chief Digital Officer at LVMH

In Chap. 5, we discussed different aspects of personalisation on the product, service and communication levels, such as personalised marketing ads and personalised e-mail communication from a sales associate; individual storefronts and wish lists; personalised content and experiences; co-browsing, co-design and co-creation of products; products with a unique history and transparent origin; individual appointment booking; delivery to suit personal preferences; the value of personal recommendations and personalised customer services. Different tools were described in that chapter. The omni-channel continues to operate as the basis for the omni-personal strategy. The particular challenge here is the seamless and sustainable transformation of the existing IT and logistics systems. The number of processes and channels required influences the complexity associated with this task. The central integration of Enterprise Resource Planning (ERP), CRM, CMS, analytics and other tools is becoming a key success factor. The omni-personal experience builds on this foundation.

Necessity is the mother of invention, so technology is constantly evolving to provide better tools for better experiences. The omni-personal approach is no exception to that rule. Once the business and operating models have been defined, the market potential is estimated, the right talent is hired and the technology is selected to amortise the investment.

The holistic requirement gathering usually takes place within a dedicated assessment involving stakeholders from a business and a technical perspective. In addition, existing legacy technologies might cause further complexity that needs to be considered and estimated. The technology selection depends on the business and technical requirements for the overall target architecture.

Aspects like the scope of out-of-the-box functionalities, scalability, extendability, flexibility, interfaces, experience and budget play a special role in that view. Moreover, the involvement of third parties, such as hosting or maintenance support, as is typically stipulated in a service-level agreement, is an important element to be defined in a contract.

Cloud Solutions to Act in Real Time with the Customer

The contract should also include the licensing model, which differentiates between the following:

- *On-premises* means that a company owns software and hosts it on its own servers. From implementation to maintenance, the company fully owns and controls the solution. All tasks are carried out internally as long as no third parties are required for certain aspects.
- *Cloud* solutions are subscription-based on-demand computer system resources for larger companies. A cloud service provider or third party manages the hosting of the software, and data are more flexible and accessible at any time in the cloud. While the private cloud set-up allows full control and customisation (operating system, software, data, administration, user accounts and settings), a shared cloud set-up stores data from different subscribers on the same server, granting complete privacy to each of them. According to the company's needs, you define the location of the remote servers and allocate them worldwide. Correspondingly, you simplify the IT infrastructure and required in-house IT know-how.
- *Software as a service (SaaS) and platform as a service (PaaS)* are subtypes of cloud computing, tailored as inexpensive subscription solutions for selected operations. An already-developed cloud-based solution is accessible online. However, the control possibilities for a company are limited to user accounts and settings.

In an omni-personal world, real-time data synchronisation and access matter to the ability to monitor customer interactions and transactions seamlessly across channels. This is necessary to enable a company to react in real time and in a customer-relevant manner. Therefore, a cloud-based approach is vital whenever possible as it unlocks flexibility and results in short go-to-market times.

CMS, DAM and PIM to Communicate Consistently with the Customer

- *CMS* stands for content management system; such a system supports collaborative content creation and the editing, publishing and deleting of websites. A CMS builds on templates and comprehensive editors to adjust building blocks easily.
- *DAM* is the abbreviation for digital asset management, which offers a central unified library of media elements from images to 3D objects and from audio files to videos. A catalogue of resizing, editing, searching and security features is available.
- *PIM* means product information management and centralises product-related data registration and maintenance from the product title to the

description, supplier information and even product images. It is possible to manage multi-language translations as well.

From an omni-personal perspective, the combination of CMS, DAM and PIM ensures that the right product image size and resolution are always displayed in the right channel and with the product description in the appropriate language. On a product detail page, it is vital to show the correct product data and ensure consistent communication. This is especially important for fully personalised marketing campaigns or landing pages: after login, individual recommendations are compiled based on the personal wish list and colour and style preferences. Linking visuals to certain customer segments and campaigns requires a crystal-clear and scalable categorisation and tagging logic. Moreover, process flows are imperative to guarantee quality checks.

Analytics to Understand the Customer
As outlined in Sect. 5.6 in Chap. 5, analytics is essential to monitoring and understanding customer behaviour to enable better decision making based on signals tracked along the customer journey.

- *Internal data* are available from different channels, like websites, e-commerce, retail and wholesale, social media, in-store traffic tracking and marketing tools like Google AdWords or newsletter performance.
- *External data* enrich the internal data with market data, sales channel insights, socio-demographic information and social listening. The best mix depends on the business question, data availability and even geographic limitations. In data-rich countries, it is easy to retrieve data via consumer panels, POS data monitored by payment service providers or industry studies powered by syndicates. In data-poor countries, access panels are typically set up to survey customers once or recurrently. New data sources, like clickstream analysis and social media, can open up rich insights into customer behaviour, such as major keywords, device preferences and searching or buying patterns.

In an omni-personal interpretation, the data from different sources need to be aggregated and translated from big data into smart data to gain a complete picture of the current status and potential growth areas. It is particularly important to optimise the customer segmentation with these insights. That is where a customer data platform (CDP) stands out as it consolidates master platform data streams from different channels and tools, including order management system (OMS) and CRM. It is the natural extension of CRM tools.

CRM to Manage the Relationship with the Customer
One central CRM or CDP with a 360-degree view of the customer is at the heart of omni-personal experiences. It prevents organisational amnesia and allows empathic relationship building, regardless of the customer's location, language or culture. Beyond classical CRM tools and features like customer creation, editing and deletion across channels, a CDP platform is made to unlock a complete view of a firm's customers across channels (see also Sect. 5.6 in Chap. 5).

Whether CRM or CDP, at least one unique identifier needs to be assigned to every customer to create the golden record in both cases. This identifier is necessary to merge personal and transactional data, captured via different channels, into one master customer data set. This is typically the most recent client data aggregation with the highest completeness score. As soon as a new client data set is registered, the system checks in real time the information entered automatically in duplicated and new data fields. It also identifies data that include typos or are very close to an existing data entry. Just imagine a street name that can be written once with 'blanc' and once without. Such fields are deduplicated.

Now imagine the new data entry for a customer who purchased a new watch. You might be interested to see the sales action in proportion to the customer's purchase frequency and the average purchase amount. A dedicated scoring model takes different factors into account. You can merge data fields based on formulas, aggregation or scoring rules. Alternatively, you can define field values via 'select'. That applies, for example, when you think about legal compliance with the General Data Privacy Regulation (GDPR). You are legally obliged to ensure that you capture and reflect the most recent customer marketing consent. By default, the system should take the most recent data entry into account.

All individual data entries and their sources remain accessible and linked to the golden record. Consequently, the CRM or CDP platform provides a clear view of the sales and transaction history of a customer across channels and supports customer segmentation, which is necessary for personalised marketing and communication across touchpoints.

6.2.2 Processes Ensure Seamless Omni-personal Experiences

You can have the best strategy in the world, the difference between the excellent and the incompetent is execution, execution, execution.
 —Domenico De Sole, Former CEO at Gucci Group

Looking at the omni-personal processes as part of the operating model, structured processes and transparent communication enable seamless operations. The equation is simple: the best technology is useless unless it is integrated into the right processes. These are divided into three phases: target definition, change management and governance to make the processes evergreen once they have been defined.

First and foremost, the target processes need to be defined and documented to reach the target picture embedding technologies. At the same time, the roles and responsibilities need to be clarified as well as the process ownership.

New omni-personal processes need to ensure seamless collaboration across company departments, like marketing, content, communications, sales, customer relationship management, customer service and analytics, which have potentially acted independently in the past. This is one of the major challenges in luxury. Obviously, siloed thinking and acting make no sense in an omni-personal set-up. The 'click' and the 'brick' should belong to one world and one experience. Cross-functional teams unlock the necessary efficiency on behalf of the customer and simplify the application of a test-and-learn approach. Instant sharing of insights is a prerequisite for personalisation at scale. This translates into a significant cultural shift for traditionally organised companies and demands change management and sufficient training.

Collaboration calls for communication to keep the governance evergreen. Every stakeholder is involved in regular meetings and alignment routines to ensure continuous reflection, progress and success of the transformation. To address the high dynamic in the omni-personal transformation context, a process-oriented perspective and an agile delivery and risk mitigation approach are strongly recommended. The customer orientation must be dynamic as customer behaviour itself is not a static constant. The same customer who said A and B twice suddenly says C during the third contact. The delivery methodology should allow certain flexibility. Thanks to technological development and multiple performance measurement possibilities, agility is an important success factor for continuous improvement processes. This does not mean just that new software releases are deployed in every sprint but that the respective teams are allowed to act in a self-determined manner within the scope of their responsibilities.

Briefly, omni-personal processes need to work like a Swiss clock. However, the process of implementing the omni-personal needs to leave degrees of freedom to react to new technological developments and new insights generated from iterative feedback loops with customers. Ultimately, the team driving the organisation towards the omni-personal needs to have a certain agility in innovation along the way.

6.2.3 People with the Right Skills and Expertise Drive the Change

Some people love to repeat the past. But you don't create when you repeat.
—Jean-Claude Biver, Former Chairman at Hublot

Change management calls for smooth processes, the right talent, customer-centric thinking and the ability to train others in the new culture, processes and tools. An organisation needs to ensure that people with the right skills, experience and expertise are on board. It is self-explanatory that a company should support its existing employees in their development of new skills, but potentially, they are not yet experienced in omni-personal transformation management. To gain that experience, outside talent is recruited as internal employees or consulted as external experts.

The omni-personal team will require completely new skill sets adjusted to the new set-up. That calls for digital natives: marketeers, data scientists and people who live in the cloud. New skills also necessitate a new environment encouraging innovation and outside-the-box thinking. That refers to a kind of studio-style start-up set-up in which new ideas have grounds and a future.

Incentives and gamification are smart ways to build engagement and enthusiasm for new concepts. You think that a happy customer should be convincing enough as a positive reward. Maybe you are right. Nevertheless, why not use all the levers?

Commission models and incentives in the form of bonuses and commission are often linked to a single channel's success. This favours the cannibalisation effect, which is not a good practice in either an omni-channel or an omni-personal context. Therefore, framework conditions must be created in which the brand, and not the channel, is in the spotlight. As already mentioned in relation to processes, omni-channel excellence requires a cultural change within an organisation. Flat hierarchies and a culture of knowledge sharing are imperative as well.

Gamification is important to keep in mind because every customer experience is designed by people. Guess what? An employee with a limited view has a tough time opening up new horizons for customers. An employee who has no fun at work faces mission impossible when asked to trigger enthusiasm in customers. This is where gamification prompts internal learning and sharing. It is as easy as collecting badges for special commitment, achievements, skills and expertise. Visualised praise gives the energy needed for the next extra mile. The keyword is 'dopamine', which is released when a person challenges himself or herself and achieves the desired target. That is the formula of pleasure and calls for repetition.[1] A playful environment supports efficiency and individual joy at work and continuous learning. Of course, it does not compensate for a lack of technology or processes.

Finally, the enthusiasm and encouragement that inspire employees radiate to the outside world. This statement crystallises when we realise that employees are the most important touchpoint with customers, accounting for 32 per cent, followed by product tests, search engines and advertising.[2]

6.3 Three Emerging Approaches to the Omni-personal Strategy

On several occasions in this book, we have described the omni-channel as the basis for the omni-personal strategy. Within the next chapter, we will focus on an e-commerce perspective. Basically, three roads lead to Rome. The approaches are:

- Vertically integrated
- Modular marketplace or e-retail
- Full-stack ecosystem

6.3.1 A Vertically Integrated Approach Allows Full Control

Hermès and Gucci are doing it, as well as Bulgari. Do you know the saying 'If you want to do it well, do it yourself'? That is, in a figurative sense, the logic behind the vertically integrated approach. In simple terms, you create the e-commerce solution yourself and consequently gain maximum control. When a brand opts for that approach, it adopts a mono-brand omni-personal architecture. To meet the requirements of this architecture, Breitling, for example, puts digital transformation at the heart of its operating model.[3] Accordingly, it focuses not on individual initiatives but on holistic thinking and action in its digital ecosystem.

The mono-brand architecture is mainly used by large brands with high revenue volumes. The reason is simple: building your own online shop and maintaining it are expensive—whether in house or outsourced. In return, these big players, like SAP Hybris, Intershop and Magento, offer omni-channel structures and out-of-the-box features, which would have to be developed at additional expense in house.

Certainly, having full control of your own e-commerce system is tempting, particularly in respect of customer access. Those who do not operate their own online shop could lose a relationship with a growing customer segment in the long run. Of course, a brand on YNAP or Farfetch owns the customer data, but the real winner is the platform, which learns about customers' cross-brand shopping patterns. These data are the new gold.

Furthermore, in your own online shop, you do not pay commission on your sales. However, you pay for licences and maintenance. The trick here is to find the right e-commerce platform for your needs and requirements to avoid overinvesting in an over- or underdimensioned system—briefly, the wrong system. That is why the proper requirement gathering is so important.

Well, you may think, the way of Hermès is not your way, and you are looking for a more flexible way to activate and scale e-commerce.

6.3.2 A Modular Marketplace or e-Retail Approach Provides Partial Control

Considering that the best way is to start small, the modular marketplace or e-retail approach could offer a better fit. In that context, the leading third-party multi-brand marketplace Farfetch or the e-retailer YNAP cannot be avoided. Moreover, 24S (previously 24 Sèvres, named after the address of 'Le Bon Marché'), Mytheresa and Luisa Via Roma represent successful multi-brand online retail cases. In recent years, they have grown rapidly. However, most platforms focus on fashion. Today, Net-a-Porter lists jewellery and watch brands and Farfetch partners with selected hard luxury brands like Boucheron.

This implies that a good share of the jewellery and watch business belongs to the retail and wholesale channel with partners à la Bucherer, Wempe, Timevallée and so on. Rolex, for instance, has been known until today as

Bucherer's most important partner. The online channel here clearly acts as the first touchpoint with the brand, but the sales ceremony remains a people business.

As a less-known brand, you might see more benefit in the modular marketplace or the e-retail platform effects. In other words, the brand and its products are listed side by side with other brands and products. This allows comparison but also a broader reach. In return, all brands benefit from the customer traffic and have their fair chance to convince. The platform provider is in charge of generating traffic and qualified leads to benefit from the sales margin or commission.

In the marketplace case of Farfetch, traditional independent retailers list their products online via API. Once a product is sold online, Farfetch earns the commission. The retailer prepares the package, adds the shipment label provided by Farfetch and sends the product to the customer via drop shipping. Same-day delivery and click and collect are supported. Farfetch remains in charge of the 24/7 customer service as the first point of contact for the customer. In the case of a return, the customer chooses between returning a product online and returning it in store.

In contrast, YNAP is a classical e-retailer that controls the entire value chain from buying inventory via the brand and 3D product presentation to fulfilment, fast delivery and customer relationship management. Initially, the platform served its customers via drop shipping, but since then it has built its own international warehouses.

These cases are similar but different: multi-brand flash-sale platforms like Vente-Privée are not relevant to the pure jewellery and watch brand context but act as an interesting option for internal staff sales within brands and conglomerates. Due to the limited quantity available and the time constraints, this concept falls under the marketplace option with partial control. Social live-commerce platforms like Tmall Luxury Pavilion are a kind of new interpretation of flash-sale platforms. They extend the principle successfully to increase brand awareness among young generations.

Third-party multi-brand retailers, flash-sale platforms and social commerce platforms offer brands online sales channels but no full control over the brand and product presentation, the packaging and the delivery experience. The contract terms include fixed run times and exclusivity clauses, which should be borne in mind by a brand. If that does not hold you back, it is time to cut the whole cake.

6.3.3 Leveraging the Full-Stack Ecosystem Approach Creates Lock-In Effects

The full-stack ecosystem approach in luxury is targeted via third-party mono-brand retail or as a platform shareholder, the latter being the cherry on the cake. It stands for the luxury way in the luxury business.

YNAP operates 41 and Farfetch Black & White Platform Solutions 8 luxury mono-brand stores.[4] We understand third-party mono-brand retail as an extension of multi-brand marketplaces or e-retailers, offering luxury brands exclusive white-label solutions. Farfetch and YNAP leverage their ecosystem to build synergies and to accelerate the go-to-market time for brands. Brands benefit from the digital toolbox and omni-channel expertise of digital-first platforms without building the technology and infrastructure themselves. This is less expensive because the platform provider develops new shared features more efficiently than each brand would be able to realise on its own.

Are you wondering about the deal? The brand pays for maintenance support and the website and online shop building that are based on a classical CMS, including the integration of a mobile app. The design phase gives the brand freedom to propose a brand-consistent layout and define the product order within the catalogue. Technically speaking, the solution is API based, allowing the brand to synchronise the online shop's inventory data with data from stores and warehouses across the network.

We do not want to repeat the full list of platform features available, adjustable to brands' needs in a modular way. More importantly, we outline the international payment handling, international delivery via click and collect or in-store returns, RFID technology, multi-lingual storefronts and integration of WeChat mini programmes. Brands even have the option to outsource services like content production or a brand-trained customer service team. Analytic dashboards are configured in tools like Tableau to control and visualise the performance, acting as the basis of regular business reviews between platform provider and brand.

You assume correctly that innovation gains the lion's share. Beyond omni-channel e-commerce, YNAP and Farfetch invest in ongoing innovation, including the acquisition of niche specialists to build new phygital capabilities. Farfetch's open-minded approach allows brands and retailers to use third-party technologies via their platform.[5] CuriosityChina, for example, belongs to Farfetch and helps luxury brands to succeed with WeChat in China. Another example is Certona, an AI-based personalisation capability provider.

The strategic partnership with Farfetch unlocks personalised content, searching and product recommendations in real time across touchpoints for all Black & White customers. This improves customer conversion, engagement and, finally, an improved customer lifetime value.[6]

In 2017, YNAP teamed up to build an AI-backed omni-channel 'Next Era' business model enabling inventory transparency across fulfilment centres and stores.[7] Moreover, the model allows extended in-store services, such as quick check-out, click and collect, return in store, live chat assistance and on-site personalisation.

Farfetch conjured another rabbit out of the hat and launched the 'Store of the Future'. This augmented reality project aims to optimise the interaction between the customer and the sales associate across channels. Thomas Browne started to pilot the technology in its stores in 2018. In the same year, Chanel teamed up with Farfetch to work on innovative cross-channel initiatives for luxurious customer experiences. This leads us seamlessly to platform shareholding.

Chanel is indeed more than an innovation partner. The iconic brand holds a minority stake in Farfetch. This strategic investment is thought to improve Chanel's customer service and excludes online selling. Considering the acquisition of YNAP by luxury conglomerate Richemont, it is obvious that this was motivated by a much more holistic strategy and vision to become the leading omni-channel player in luxury and fashion and to grant exclusivity to the conglomerate-controlled brands. M&As, joint ventures and strategic partnering with digital platforms or niche experts are interesting options to accelerate the omni-personal transformation in an ecosystem environment.

Finally, let us ensure that we have a common understanding of an ecosystem: an ecosystem is based on a collaborative customer relationship. The customer and provider engage in continuous data exchange to achieve the maximum benefit. Like a shared house, the platform becomes the indispensable link that enables coexistence and exchange.

An ecosystem's service spectrum can and should be diverse to keep the user happy and satisfied with the range of services offered. A well-known example is Amazon, which offers everything from *The Big Book of Cooking* to music subscriptions, Amazon Pay or storage space in the cloud. A hacked Amazon account may therefore cause the same pain as having your house burgled.

Moving to another platform is costly and time consuming—and you need to be convinced about your decision. On the one hand, an ecosystem raises the barriers to market entry and thus protects you from competitors. On the other hand, a strong-performance ecosystem binds its customers in the long term. This is due to the network effect: the more users invest in a platform, the more a platform is able to reinvest in new functionalities. This positive resonance is the famous win-win that we often crave. Why then do we want something new and different? The consequence of this is that it pays to be quick. Once you have furnished your house, painted the built-in wardrobe moss green and found the weekly domestic help thanks to various advertisements, then you experience the lock-in effect. You will think twice about the added value and benefits of a potential second home, and leaving your home becomes an option only if the leading ecosystem fails.

Next: How do you know what is the right approach for your business?

6.4 The Approach Depends on Brand Reach and Control

Digital luxury customers are increasingly seeking a multi-brand experience.[8] The winners seem to be those brands that are building scalable models to grow and evolve into ecosystems, providing their creations direct to the customer (D2C) and via third-party platforms. However, each brand size and maturity level calls for its own approach, and again, there is not just one method (Fig. 6.4).

APPROACH	DISTINCTION	KEY ADVANTAGES/DISADVANTAGES	
		Control	Reach
Vertically integrated	Mono-brand architecture	++	0
Modular marketplace or e-retail	Multi-brand flash sale	--	+
	Multi-brand social commerce	--	++
	Third-party multi-brand marketplace/e-retail	-	++
Full-stack ecosystem	Third-party mono-brand retail	+	0
	Platform shareholder	++	+

0 neutral; + advantage; - disadvantage

Fig. 6.4 The intended brand reach and control define the approach

If you are a smaller brand with lower reach, you can find the perfect starting point with a modular marketplace or e-retail to pilot the e-commerce channel for your business. The minimal brand control over the flash sale and social commerce initiatives makes both appropriate for brand awareness campaigns to reach new young target groups, particularly in Asia. Hence, a third-party multi-brand marketplace or e-retail should be the first port of call for brands looking for a certain degree of control combined with additional reach thanks to the platform effect. That set-up allows brands to grow and scale the business together with the platform up to the point at which a mono-brand architecture becomes relevant. The possible level of personalisation is restricted in that first phase.

Moving forward, the mono-brand architecture unlocking the direct-to-customer (D2C) approach is usually realised as an add-on or stand-alone solution. As a brand, you need to choose between vertical in-house integration and the white-label mono-brand offering of a third-party ecosystem. Of course, a brand with high reach would directly jump to the decision to build up in-house omni-channel capabilities rather than outsourcing to third-party platforms. In that phase, omni-personalisation at scale is typically addressed via third-party software integration.

You are a big brand or conglomerate with significant reach and revenue streams, so you consider investing in building up your own ecosystem to achieve the maximum control. The full-stack ecosystem reduces your external dependencies since you optimise and scale synergies along the value chain following a customer-centric logic.

In summary, all the approaches have their justification and business case. The business case differs from brand to brand and can therefore be analysed and evaluated only individually. There is no one-size-fits-all solution. What is right for Buccellati is not necessarily right for Van Cleef & Arpels, even though both are jewellers and belong to the same conglomerate. The same applies to LVMH: the conglomerate centralises technology, CRM, clienteling and analytics on the group level while the e-commerce maturity varies between brands.[9]

It is crucial to question the function and structure of a brand's business model conceptually and reconfigure it in a future-proof way. A prerequisite is, of course, a clear view of the growth potential linked to omni-personalisation.

Notes

1. Zichermann G, Linder J (2013) The gamification revolution: how leaders leverage game mechanics to crush the competition. McGraw-Hill Education, New York, p 218.
2. Goldhausen K (2018) Customer Experience Management—wie man Kunden begeistern kann. In: Rusnjak A, Schallmo R (eds) Customer Experience im Zeitalter des Kunden: Best Practices, Lessons Learned und Forschungsergebnisse. Springer, Wiesbaden, pp 193–241.
3. Batat W (2019) The new luxury experience: creating the ultimate customer experience. Springer, Wiesbaden, Location 3251.
4. Woodworth S (2019) Why luxury brands build their online retail with monobrand platforms. https://luxe.digital/business/digital-luxury-reports/luxury-brands-use-third-party-platforms-build-online-monobrand-stores/. Accessed 6 September 2020.
5. Farfetch (2021) Company homepage. https://aboutfarfetch.com/about/farfetch-platform-solutions/ & https://aboutfarfetch.com/about/store-of-the-future/. Accessed 8 January 2021.
6. Strzalek A (2017) Certona & Farfetch in online personalisation deal. https://www.retail-systems.com/rs/Certona_Farfetch_Personalisation_Deal.php. Accessed 23 August 2020.
7. Yoox-Net-A-Porter Group (2017) Valentino and Yoox-Net-A-Porter join forces to create an innovative blueprint for the next era of luxury retail. https://www.ynap.com/news/valentino-and-yoox-net-a-porter-group-join-forces-to-create-an-innovative-blueprint-for-the-next-era-of-luxury-retail/. Accessed 7 April 2020.
8. McKinsey & Company (2018) The age of digital Darwinism. https://www.mckinsey.com/~/media/McKinsey/Industries/Retail/Our%20Insights/Luxury%20in%20the%20age%20of%20digital%20Darwinism/The-age-of-digital-Darwinism.pdf, p 9. Accessed 3 April 2021.
9. Guiltbault L (2020) LVMH and Kering's new battlefield is online. https://www.voguebusiness.com/companies/lvmh-and-kerings-new-battlefield-is-online-covid-19. Accessed 12 June 2020.

7

Conclusion: Embark on Your Journey to the Omni-personal Now

Can you remember all the birthdays of your important customers? Monsieur Cartier or Mademoiselle Chanel probably could. Can you remember all the birthdays of your friends? What about the birthdays of your colleagues? We say, 'Thank you, LinkedIn and Facebook, as you remind us every day about the birthdays, achievements and latest news'. They have replaced many handwritten birthday planners and allowed us to send more personal congratulations. In private, we have started to manage our personal contacts at scale—without great pain and with much or little strategy. On an organisational level, we experience the same psychological effects. Omni-personalisation leads to increased loyalty.

Who is not happy when someone thinks of them on their birthday? It gives us positive emotions—even more so if we share a common history, presence or plans for the future. Big changes are challenging, but sometimes they appear natural, like our desire to wish our friends and colleagues a happy day. For a company, that positive emotion translates into loyalty and leads to growth and profitability. Luxury has proven many times that the industry is able to reinvent itself. Today, it has another chance to prove that flexibility. We are coming to the end of this book and the beginning of your action.

It does not matter whether you are a big player or a small- or medium-sized brand. Everything described in this book is valid and applicable independently of the current maturity and reach of your brand. Therefore, we encourage you to take the first step. Please do not wait until your company becomes a large one or until the world has changed—we are experiencing a continuous change, and the only way to address it is never stopping to start and never starting to stop. The omni-personal is a journey and definitely a way to grow thanks to trusted and relevant relationships between your brand and your customers.

The journey starts by assessing your organisation's omni-personal maturity. Such an assessment allows you to identify potentials and prioritise them to make your brand ready for the future. This involves five steps:

1. Understand your current situation in terms of the customer journey, processes, tools and people.
2. Define your target situation in terms of the customer journey, processes, tools and people.
3. Identify and prioritise gaps to be closed and derive actions to be taken.
4. Develop your omni-personal transformation roadmap.
5. Kick off your journey towards the omni-personal.

Knowing that many companies are still challenged by the omni-channel, this book envisions the omni-personal future for an industry that is deeply rooted in personalisation. This can be broken down into 'go back to your roots and integrate new retail principles and technologies'. Monsieur Cartier or Mademoiselle Chanel would smile.

Dear reader, we hope that we have inspired you and answered your essential questions about who, why, how, what and when the omni-personal approach matters most in luxury. You have seen manifold ways to realise personalisation at scale along the customer journey, including the personalisation of the product, the service, the communication and the experience. However, we are aware that there is still much to do to make the omni-personal vision a reality. Additional questions will arise during that transformation. Further customer expectations will evolve and new technologies will be derived, leading to innovation to meet the expectations.

Take it competitive.

Take it omni-personal.

Your customer will thank you.

Bibliography

Abtan O, Barton C (2016) Digital or die: the choice for luxury brands. www.bcg.com/publications/2016/digital-or-die-choice-luxury-brands.aspx. Accessed 20 October 2020.

Accenture (2020) Accenture and Microsoft collaborate to provide digital platform to support Camera Nazionale Della Moda Italiana's Milan digital fashion week. https://newsroom.accenture.com/news/accenture-and-microsoft-collaborate-to-provide-digital-platform-to-support-camera-nazionale-della-moda-italianas-milan-digital-fashion-week.htm. Accessed 14 July 2020.

Accenture (2021) Virtual showcase by Accenture. https://www.youtube.com/watch?v=JZPcSg-9Swc. Accessed 18 March 2021.

Achille A (2019) McKinsey and Altagamma—win big in digital. Altagamma. https://altagamma.it/media/source/turtl-story-nAcnMU_1.pdf. Accessed 10 December 2020.

Achille A, Zipser D (2020) A perspective for the luxury-goods industry during—and after—coronavirus. https://www.mckinsey.com/industries/retail/our-insights/a-perspective-for-the-luxury-goods-industry-during-and-after-coronavirus. Accessed 1 April 2020.

Adresta (2020) Company website. https://adresta.ch/en. Accessed 31 December 2020.

Altiant (2019) New models of luxury ownership: resale, rentals & subscriptions. https://altiant.com/new-models-of-luxury-ownership, p 9. Accessed 30 November 2020.

Aminoff J (2016) Social selling luxury: increase sales by engaging in the digital world. Luxury Sales Academy.

Arianee (2021) Company website. https://www.arianee.org. Accessed 28 February 2021.

Bain & Company (2020) Bain-Altagamma 2020 worldwide luxury market monitor. In: The Diamond Loupe. https://www.thediamondloupe.com/sites/awdcnews-

Bibliography

wall/files/attachments/Bain-Altagamma%20Luxury%20Study%2019th%20Edition.pdf. Accessed 18 November 2020.

Bairamian H (2018) Les marques des produits de luxe face aux medias sociaux. https://nanopdf.com/download/les-marques-des-produits-de-luxe-face-aux-medias-sociaux_pdf, p 4. Accessed 26 January 2021.

Batat W (2019a) Digital luxury. Sage Publications, Los Angeles.

Batat W (2019b) The new luxury experience: creating the ultimate customer experience. Springer, Wiesbaden, Location 3188.

Baxter N (2019) 7 ways fashion brands are harnessing hologram technology. https://thecurrentdaily.com/2019/10/01/7-ways-fashion-brands-are-harnessing-hologram-technology/. Accessed 1 October.

Beauloye F (2017) SHINE: digital craftsmanship for modern luxury brands. Michael Hanrahan, Singapore.

Bezamat B (2018) Hermès launches mobile game as part of year-long celebration of play. https://thecurrentdaily.com/2018/03/28/hermes-mobile-game-play/. Accessed 28 March 2020.

Binkley C (2021) Private broadcasts are luxury brands' new secret weapon. https://www.voguebusiness.com/companies/private-broadcasts-are-luxury-brands-new-secret-weapon. Accessed 17 March 2021.

Böckenholt I, Mehn A (eds) (2018) Konzepte und Strategien für Omnichannel-Exzellenz: Innovatives Retail-Marketing mit mehrdimensionalen Vertriebs- und Kommunikationskanälen. Springer, Wiesbaden.

Bourdieu P (1985) A social critique of the judgement of taste. Harvard University Press, Cambridge.

Breitling (2020) Company website. https://www.breitling.com/de-de/service/blockchain/. Accessed 31 December 2020.

Brighton, Reichheld F (1996) The loyalty effect: the hidden force behind growth, profits, and lasting value. Harvard Business School Press, Brighton.

British Museum (2020) How to explore the British Museum from home. https://blog.britishmuseum.org/how-to-explore-the-british-museum-from-home/. Accessed 27 March 2020.

Canaves S (2020) Hard luxury gets the livestreaming treatment. https://jingdaily.com/hard-luxury-gets-the-livestreaming-treatment. Accessed 30 April 2020.

Cartier Brickell F (2019) The Cartiers: the untold story of the family behind the jewellery empire. Random House, New York.

Caula R (2013) Ross Lovegrove 3D prints gold rings for Louisa Guinness Gallery. https://www.designboom.com/design/ross-lovegrove-3d-prints-18k-gold-rings-for-louisa-guinness-gallery-11-30-2013/. Accessed 30 November 2020.

Chadha R, Husband P (2006) The cult of the luxury brand: inside Asia's love affair with luxury. Nicholas Brealey International, London.

Chang A, Mauron P (2020) JingDigital and Digital Luxury Group—WeChat luxury index 2020. JingDigital. https://www.jingdigital.com/en/articles/8255/, p 2, 50. Accessed 3 April 2021.

Bibliography

Changsha IFS (2020) Changsha IFS creates iGO, the first MR shopping navigator in China, to open smart shopping with one click. In: Cision PR Newswire. https://www.prnewswire.com/news-releases/changsha-ifs-entwickelt-igo-den-ersten-mr-einkaufsnavigator-in-china-der-intelligentes-einkaufen-mit-einem-klick-ermoglicht-819629444.html. Accessed 16 December 2020.

Chaumet (2021) Company homepage. https://inimitablejosephine.chaumet.com/en/. Accessed 28 March 2021.

Chevalier M, Gutsatz M (eds) (2019) Luxury retail and digital management. Wiley, New Jersey.

Chopard (2020) Company website. https://www.chopard.com/intl/green-carpet-collection. Accessed 2 August 2020.

ConsenSys (2019) LVMH, ConsenSys, and Microsoft announce consortium for luxury industry. https://consensys.net/blog/press-release/lvmh-microsoft-consensys-announce-aura-to-power-luxury-industry/. Accessed 16 May 2020.

Corbellini E, Saviolo S (2014) Managing fashion and luxury companies. Rizzoli Etas, Milan.

Corder R (2018) Swiss watchmaker tracks timepieces for life using blockchain technology. https://www.watchpro.com/swiss-watchmaker-tracks-timepieces-for-life-using-blockchain-technology/. Accessed 24 September 2020.

Corzine M (2020) Philips Watches Head of Digital Strategy: 'Collectors were quick to accept digital sales'. https://www.luxurysociety.com/en/articles/2020/06/phillips-watches-head-digital-strategy-collectors-were-quick-accept-digital-sales/. Accessed 25 June 2020.

Cumenal F (2017) How I did it: Tiffany's CEO on creating a sustainable supply chain. Harvard Business Review. March–April:41–46.

Danziger P (2019) Meet the HENRYS: the millennials that matter most for luxury. Paramount Market Publishing, Ithaca.

Daugherty P, Wilson H (2018) Human + machine: reimagining work in the age of AI. Harvard Business Review, Boston.

Doerr E (2016) Jaeger-LeCoultre joins forces with shoe designer Christian Louboutin on Atelier Reverso line. https://www.forbes.com/sites/elizabethdoerr/2016/01/26/jaeger-lecoultre-joins-forces-with-shoe-designer-christian-louboutin-on-atelier-reverso-line/#607bcfa7fdc2. Accessed 26 January 2021.

Doran S (2011) 11 fine jewellery designers, China & Taiwan. https://www.luxurysociety.com/en/articles/2011/11/11-fine-jewellery-designers-china-taiwan/. Accessed 25 November 2020.

Dudarenok AG, Zakkour M (2019) New retail born in China going global: how Chinese tech giants are changing global commerce. Independently published.

Entrupy (2020) Company website. https://www.entrupy.com. Accessed 31 December 2020.

EOS (2012) Glänzende Aussichten mit additiver Fertigung von Gold. https://www.eos.info/01_parts-and-applications/case_studies_applications_parts/_case_studies_pdf/de_cases/cs_m_cookson_gold_cpm.pdf. Accessed 1 November 2021.

Bibliography

Estève C (2016) Understanding luxury through Maslow's hierarchy of needs. https://www.agora.universite-paris-saclay.fr/understanding-luxury-through-maslows-hierarchy-of-needs/. Accessed 21 November 2020.

Everledger (2020) Company website. https://www.everledger.io/case-study/everledger-with-gia-and-chow-tai-fook/. Accessed 27 December 2020.

Facebook (2020) Introducing Facebook shops: helping small businesses sell online. https://about.fb.com/news/2020/05/introducing-facebook-shops/. Accessed 19 May 2020.

Farfetch (2021) Company homepage. https://aboutfarfetch.com/about/farfetch-platform-solutions/ & https://aboutfarfetch.com/about/store-of-the-future/. Accessed 8 January 2021.

Gardetti MÁ, Coste-Manière I (eds) (2020) Sustainable luxury and craftsmanship: environmental footprints and eco-design of products and processes. Springer Nature Singapore Pte Ltd, Singapore.

Gartner (2019) Lessons from luxury retail—younger generation lead the way. https://www.gartner.com/en/documents/3905168/lessons-from-luxury-retail-younger-generations-lead-the-. Accessed 20 March.

GMA MarketingToChina (2020) Golden rules to social media marketing in China (updated 2020). https://www.marketingtochina.com/golden-rules-to-social-media-marketing-in-china-updated-2019/. Accessed 4 February 2021.

Goldhausen K (2018) Customer Experience Management—wie man Kunden begeistern kann. In: Rusnjak A, Schallmo R (eds) Customer Experience im Zeitalter des Kunden: best practices, lessons learned und Forschungsergebnisse. Springer, Wiesbaden.

Google Trends (2021) 'Engagement ring' versus 'Cartier ring' in the last 12 months. https://trends.google.de/trends/explore?q=engagement%20ring,cartier%20ring. Accessed 14 March 2021.

GQ (2020) Rolex der Zukunft? Technischer Durchbruch könnte aus Luxusuhren eine Smartwatch machen. https://www.gq-magazin.de/mode/artikel/rolex-der-zukunft-technischer-durchbruch-macht-luxusuhren-zu-smartwatch. Accessed 5 August 2020.

Guiltbault L (2020a) Jewellery spending is down. It's still a good bet. https://www.voguebusiness.com/companies/jewellery-spending-is-down-its-still-a-good-bet. Accessed 3 July 2020.

Guiltbault L (2020b) LVMH and Kering's new battlefield is online. https://www.voguebusiness.com/companies/lvmh-and-kerings-new-battlefield-is-online-covid-19. Accessed 12 June 2020.

Hall C (2020) Weibo enters the e-commerce race. Should brands be excited or cautious? https://www.businessoffashion.com/articles/professional/weibo-enters-e-commerce-race-should-brands-be-excited-or-cautious. Accessed 4 May 2020.

Hapticmedia (2020) Configure your watch in 3D. https://hapticmedia.fr/en/clients-projects/3d-configurator-watch-baume/. Accessed 21 December 2020.

Harari Y (2013) Eine kurze Geschichte der Menschheit. Deutsche Verlags-Anstalt, Munich.

Häusel H (eds) (2016) Brain View: Warum Kunden kaufen. Haufe, Freiburg.

Heinemann G (eds) (2019) Der neue Online Handel. Springer, Wiesbaden.

Hubbard L (2019) Tiffany & Co. just opened their first men's pop-up shop in NYC. 6 December. https://www.townandcountrymag.com/style/jewelry-and-watches/a30153239/tiffany-mens-pop-up-shop-2019/.

Husemann-Kopetzky M (2018) Handbook on the psychology of pricing: 100+ effects on persuasion and influence every entrepreneur, marketer and pricing manager needs to know. Pricing School Press.

Inside Chanel (2020) Company website. https://inside.chanel.com. Accessed 31 December 2020.

Jahn M (2017) Industrie 4.0 konkret: Ein Wegweiser in die Praxis. Springer, Wiesbaden, Location 370.

Jiang Y (2020) Secoo's 24-hour livestreams on Kuaishou are a big win. https://jingdaily.com/secoo-24-hour-livestreams-on-kuaishou-are-a-big-win/. Accessed 11 June 2020.

Jiayun K (2020) Holographic installation puts jewelry in the picture. https://www.shine.cn/biz/event/2011079313/. Accessed 7 November 2020.

Jing Daily (2020) Next level livestreaming: how luxury brands can profit from China's top e-commerce trend. https://jingdaily.com/wp-content/uploads/2020/08/Next-Level-Luxury-Livestreaming-2020-Jing-Daily-CCI.pdf. Accessed 30 April 2020.

Journal Du Luxe (2020) Louis Vuitton: un mobile store dans une caravane. https://journalduluxe.fr/louis-vuitton-mobile-store-us/. Accessed 30 November.

Kapferer, J (2015) Kapferer on luxury: how luxury brands can grow yet remain rare. Kogan Page, London.

Kapferer J, Bastien V (eds) (2012) The luxury strategy: break the rules of marketing to build luxury brands. Kogan Page, London.

Kern S (2014) Wie viel ist genug? https://www.rnz.de/panorama/magazin_artikel,-Magazin-Wie-viel-ist-genug-_arid,20959.html. Accessed 26 April 2020.

Kowalsky M (2005) Johann Rupert: «Ich bin der Fluglotse der Egos». https://www.handelszeitung.ch/geld/johann-rupert-ich-bin-der-fluglotse-der-egos. Accessed 12 April 2021.

Kramer L (2010) The globe: how French innovators are putting the "social" back in social networking. Harvard Business Review. October:1–3.

Kunde J (2000) Corporate religion. Financial Times Prentice Hall, London.

Langer D (2020) How luxury brands can win during a crisis. https://jingdaily.com/how-luxury-brands-can-win-during-a-crisis. Accessed 22 April 2020.

Langer D, Heil O (2015) Luxury essentials: essential insights and strategies to manage luxury products. Center for Research on Luxury, Mainz.

LoveExploring (2018) How air travel has changed in the last 100 years. https://www.loveexploring.com/gallerylist/71818/how-air-travel-has-changed-in-the-last-100-years. Accessed 28 February 2021.

Luo J (2020) The importance of China's Gen Z men in pearl earrings. https://jingdaily.com/the-importance-of-chinas-gen-z-men-in-pearl-earrings/. Accessed 26 July 2020.

Lux T (2020) Wie in Karlsruhe mit Chrono24 der weltweit größte Marktplatz für Luxusuhren entstanden ist. https://omr.com/de/chrono24-tim-stracke-podcast/. Accessed 15 April 2020.

Luxury Daily (2018) Tiffany launches Paper Flowers in China via Tmall pop-up. https://www.luxurydaily.com/tiffany-launches-paper-flowers-in-china-via-tmall-pop-up/. Accessed 16 August 2020.

Mackevision (2019) Company website. https://www.mackevision.com/de/referenzen/oris/. Accessed 31 December 2020.

Maslow A (1943) A theory of human motivation. Psychological Review 50:370–396.

McKinsey & Company (2018) The age of digital Darwinism. https://www.mckinsey.com/~/media/McKinsey/Industries/Retail/Our%20Insights/Luxury%20in%20the%20age%20of%20digital%20Darwinism/The-age-of-digital-Darwinism.pdf. Accessed 3 April 2021.

Monteiro, F The TAG Heuer Carrera Connected Watch (A): Swiss Avant-Garde for the Digital Age, pp 11–14.

Morgan B (2019) The customer of the future: 10 guiding principles for winning tomorrow's business. Harper Collins, New York.

Nanda MC (2021) Gucci is selling $12 (virtual) sneakers. https://www.businessoffashion.com/articles/technology/gucci-is-selling-12-virtual-sneakers. Accessed 16 March.

Nason S, Salvacruz J (2017) Case study: competing against bling. Harvard Business Review. May–June:155–159.

Okonkwo U (2010) Luxury online: styles, systems, strategies. Palgrave Macmillan, Hampshire.

Opulent (2020) Company website. https://www.opulentjewelers.com/opulent-box. Accessed 29 December 2020.

Phelps N (2021) The Metaverse's first runway show is here—Watch Collina Strada, Bruce Glen, My Mum Made It, and Mowalola's IMVU Debut. https://www.vogue.com/article/imvu-virtual-fashion-show-announcement. Accessed 5 June 2021.

Pietzcker D (eds) (2018) Luxus als Distinktionsstrategie: Kommunikation in der internationalen Luxus- und Fashionindustrie. Springer, Wiesbaden.

Rambourg E (2020) Future Luxe: what's ahead for the business of luxury. Figure 1 Publishing, Berkeley.

Reichheld F (2006) The ultimate question: driving good profits and true growth. Harvard Business School Press.

Reuters (2020) New Chinese billionaires outpace U.S. by 3 to 1: Hurun. https://www.reuters.com/article/us-china-economy-wealth/new-chinese-billionaires-outpace-u-s-by-3-to-1-hurun-idUSKCN20K0YB. Accessed 26 February 2021.

Bibliography 169

Richemont (2021) Richemont consolidated financial statements. https://www.richemont.com/en/home/investors/results-reports-presentations/, p 84. Accessed 5 June 2021.

Riley D (2018) Gucci employs CR and AR experiences for spring campaign. https://thecurrentdaily.com/2018/03/01/gucci-spring2018-vr-ar-campaign/. Accessed 1 March.

Rolex (2020) Company website. https://www.rolex.org/en/rolex-awards. Accessed 2 August 2020.

Rusnjak A, Schallmo R (eds) (2018) Customer Experience im Zeitalter des Kunden: best practices, lessons learned und Forschungsergebnisse. Springer, Wiesbaden.

Santhiram S (2020) How luxury brands can leverage e-commerce to bounce back post-COVID-19. https://www.luxurysociety.com/en/articles/2020/04/how-can-luxury-brands-their-e-commerce-game-post-covid19/. Accessed 27 April 2020.

Scheier C, Held D (eds) (2012) Wie Werbung wirkt: Erkenntnisse des Neuromarketing. Haufe, Freiburg.

Sherman L (2020) The next wave of luxury e-commerce. In: The business of fashion. https://www.businessoffashion.com/education/courses/case-study-luxury-ecommerce-online-retail. Accessed 30 April 2020.

Slogans.de (2020) Slogans.de. https://www.slogans.de/slogans.php?GInput=cartier. Accessed 19 July 2020.

Spreer P (2018) PsyConversion: 101 Behavior Patterns für eine bessere User Experience und höhere Conversion -Rate im E-Commerce. Springer, Wiesbaden.

Srun F (2017) Luxury selling: lessons from the world of luxury in selling high quality goods and services to high value clients. Palgrave Macmillan, Hampshire.

Statista (2020a) Number of flights performed by the global airline industry from 2004 to 2021. https://www.statista.com/statistics/564769/airline-industry-number-of-flights/. Accessed 10 June 2020.

Statista (2020b) Number of monthly active smart device users of Tencent QQ in China from 2014 to 2019. https://www.statista.com/statistics/227352/number-of-active-tencent-im-user-accounts-in-china/. Accessed 30 April 2020.

Statista (2020c) Ranking der größten Social Networks und Messenger nach der Anzahl der Nutzer im Januar 2020. https://de.statista.com/statistik/daten/studie/181086/umfrage/die-weltweit-groessten-social-networks-nach-anzahl-der-user/. Accessed 20 January 2021.

Strzalek A (2017) Certona & Farfetch in online personalisation deal. https://www.retail-systems.com/rs/Certona_Farfetch_Personalisation_Deal.php. Accessed 23 August 2020.

Swarovski (2020) Company website. https://www.swarovski.com/en-DE/c-0311/Categories/Accessories/Cases-compatible-with-Apple-Watch-/. Accessed 2 August 2020.

Tracr (2020) Company website. https://www.tracr.com. Accessed 31 December 2020.

Vachaudez C (2021) Musy—Magnificent and Historic Natural pearl and diamond tiara. https://www.sothebys.com/en/buy/auction/2021/magnificent-jewels-and-noble-jewels-part-i/magnificent-and-historic-natural-pearl-and-diamond-2. Accessed 5 June 2021.

Vacheron Constantin (2020) Company website. https://www.vacheron-constantin.com/en2/services/impeccable-service/authenticity-certificate.html. Accessed 31 December 2020.

Veblen T (1899) The theory of the leisure class. Oxford University Press, New York.

Whiddington R (2021) Show me the Monet: MFA Boston debuts livestreaming on Kuaishou. https://jingculturecommerce.com/mfa-boston-kuaishou-international-museum-day-livestream/. Accessed 6 June 2021.

Wiesing L (eds) (2015) Luxus. Suhrkamp, Berlin.

Williams Gemma A. (2021) Will Gucci's Digital Bag Disrupt Luxury? https://jingdaily.com/gucci-roblox-dionysus-digital-fashion/. Accessed 31 May 2021.

WIseKey (2020) Company website. https://www.wisekey.com/solutions/brand-protection/authentic-customer-engagement/. Accessed 27 December 2020.

Woodworth S (2019) Why luxury brands build their online retail with monobrand platforms. https://luxe.digital/business/digital-luxury-reports/luxury-brands-use-third-party-platforms-build-online-monobrand-stores/. Accessed 6 September 2020.

Yoox-Net-A-Porter Group (2017) Valentino and Yoox-Net-A-Porter join forces to create an innovative blueprint for the next era of luxury retail. https://www.ynap.com/news/valentino-and-yoox-net-a-porter-group-join-forces-to-create-an-innovative-blueprint-for-the-next-era-of-luxury-retail/. Accessed 7 April 2020.

Zhang W, Chen J (2020) Digging for gold with data analytics at Chow Tai Fook. https://store.hbr.org/product/digging-for-gold-with-data-analytics-at-chow-tai-fook/HK1211. Accessed 3 April 2021.

Zhiwei F, Caixiong Z (2021) Changsha subway digital art museum becomes new top destination. http://www.chinadaily.com.cn/a/202104/30/WS608b75f8a31024ad0babb87e.html. Accessed 6 June 2021.

Zichermann G, Linder J (2013) The gamification revolution: how leaders leverage game mechanics to crush the competition. McGraw-Hill Education, New York.

Index[1]

A

A/B test, 130
Accenture, xvii, 10, 86
Adobe, 130, 133
Adresta, 115, 116
Advertising, 3, 27, 57, 67, 69, 73, 76, 82–84, 95, 128, 130, 134, 152
Affluent, 53
Affordable luxury, 21
After-sales, 6, 63, 67, 99, 112, 118–120, 123
Agility, 11, 145, 150, 151
AIDA, 64, 68
A. Lange & Söhne, 83
Alibaba, 7–9, 42, 45–47, 58, 60
Amazon, xvii, 4, 7, 8, 39, 48, 116, 122, 156
Analytics, 64, 66, 129, 130, 148
Android, 54, 125
API, 108, 154, 155
Apple, 39, 53, 69, 78, 88, 100, 122
Appointment-booking, 91
Arianee, 115, 125
Armani, 22
Art, 17, 18, 20, 26, 37, 54, 70, 74, 76, 78, 84, 85, 91, 96, 103
ASMR, *see* Autonomous sensory meridian response
Assessment, xii, 108, 114, 146, 162
Assortments, 109
Audemars Piguet, 23, 64, 79, 82, 84, 127
Augmented reality (AR), xix, 7, 74–76, 92, 156
Aura, 115
Authenticity, 9, 20, 26, 40, 112, 115, 122, 124, 125
Automation, 97, 108, 131
Autonomous sensory meridian response (ASMR), xix, 31, 72, 73
Avatars, 5, 80, 94

B

Bambuser, 86
Bang & Olufsen, 9, 47, 54, 72, 73
Baselworld, 72
Baume and Mercier, 101

---

[1] Note: Page numbers followed by 'n' refer to notes.

© The Author(s), under exclusive license to Springer Nature Switzerland AG 2022
R. Schmitt et al., *Omni-personal Luxury*, https://doi.org/10.1007/978-3-030-85769-1

172 Index

BEA sensors, 132
Beehivr, 86
Big data, 3, 30, 66, 127, 134, 148
Bijouets, 104
Black & White, 155, 156
Blanc de Chine, 56
Blancpain, 30
Blix, 132
Blockchain, 26, 74, 111–116, 125
Blogs, 43, 83, 95
Bloom Intelligence, 132
Bluetooth, 26, 88
Boucheron, 78, 120, 153
Breguet, 39, 95
Breitling, 10, 23, 27, 88, 96, 115, 120, 125, 153
Brunello Cucinelli, 60
Buccellati, 95, 158
Bucherer, 153
Bulgari, 26, 41, 69, 84, 95, 115, 117, 119, 128, 152
Burberry, 3, 69, 93, 100
Business model, 6, 19, 38, 39, 41, 54, 59, 104, 122, 145, 156, 158
Business unit strategy, xii, 141–144

C

Cartier, 2, 3, 7, 21, 23, 26, 32n8, 41, 70, 74, 76, 78, 82, 85, 95, 98, 111, 119, 120, 161, 162
Catalogue, 86, 104, 147, 155
CDP, *see* Customer data platform
Chanel, 9, 19, 42, 57, 58, 70, 85, 98, 119, 121, 156, 161, 162
Change management, 151
Chatbots, 91
Chaumet, 39, 78, 89, 93
China, xii, 1–3, 7, 10, 11, 20, 23, 24, 29, 42, 44, 45, 47, 48, 52, 56–58, 75, 93, 106, 117, 132, 155
Chopard, 23, 55, 84, 98, 111, 122

Chow Sang Sang, 87
Chow Tai Fook, 114–116
Christian Dior, 115
Christian Louboutin, 55
Chrono24, 40, 125
Circular economy, 2, 12, 40, 111
Click-and-collect, 90, 100, 124
Clienteling, 43, 95–97, 121, 158
Cloud, 8, 30, 54, 67, 115, 146, 147, 151, 156
CMS, *see* Content management system
Co-create, 100, 101
Collaboration, 9, 41, 47, 58, 71, 78, 114, 115, 142, 150
Comparison, 2, 20, 25, 31, 36, 40, 154
Competitive advantages, 142
Computer-generated images, 10, 72
Configuration, 5, 25, 31, 91, 98, 100–103, 105, 107, 145
ConsenSys, 115
Consistency, 5, 31, 63, 66, 67, 83
Consumption behaviour, 2, 11, 53, 59
Content management system (CMS), 67, 73, 146–148, 155
COVID-19, 1, 2, 9–12, 46–48, 56, 57, 77, 78, 92
CRM, xvii, xix, 43, 51, 52, 58, 67, 70, 71, 86, 96, 121, 129, 130, 133, 134, 145, 146, 149, 158
Cross-platform application, 127
Cryptocurrency, 80
CuriosityChina, 155
Customer-centric, 104, 110, 119, 124, 145, 151, 158
Customer data platform (CDP), xix, 67, 89, 97, 109, 110, 133, 134, 148, 149
Customer decision journey, 64
Customer journey, xii, 60, 63, 64, 66–69, 75, 88, 99, 116–117, 123, 125, 128, 130, 133, 141, 148, 162
Customer needs, 1, 8, 98
Cyreal, 73

D

DAM, *see* Digital asset management
Data analytics, 3, 134
Data management platforms, 133
De Beers, 26, 55, 116
Democratisation, 17, 21, 22, 24, 36, 118
Diamonds, 3, 18, 25, 55, 73, 83, 111, 128
Digital asset management (DAM), xix, 67, 147, 148
Digitalisation, 22, 23
Digital passport, 111
Digital twins, 72, 74, 85, 104
Digital walls, 86, 87
Digital windows, 76
Direct metal laser sintering (DMLS), xix, 105
Direct-to-customer (D2C), xix, 157, 158
Disruption, i, xii, 10, 53, 56, 60
Djula, 87
DMLS, *see* Direct metal laser sintering
DMPs, *see* Data management platforms
Drop shipping, 108, 154
D2C, *see* Direct-to-customer

E

eBay, 39–41, 47, 119
E-commerce, xvii, 1, 9, 35, 37–39, 42, 46, 47, 58, 59, 70, 86, 97, 107, 122, 148, 152, 153, 155, 158
E-mail, 67, 84, 87, 92, 96–98, 106, 119, 120, 123, 129, 146
Emotional value, 18
Empathy, 63, 66, 71
End-to-end, 132
Enterprise Resource Planning (ERP), xix, 8, 107, 146

EOS, 105
eRep, 102
E-retail platform, xii, 141
ERP, *see* Enterprise Resource Planning
Eternity, 6, 19
Ethereum, 74, 115
Everledger, 115
External data, 148

F

The Fabricant, 73
Facebook, 43, 48, 80, 161
FaceTime, 85
Farfetch, 8, 9, 23, 39, 41, 42, 58, 153–156
Fashion show, 80
Favre-Leuba, 115
FDM, *see* Fused deposition modelling
Feng Mao, 9, 58
Ferrari, 27, 100, 102, 120
Fitting room, 87
Flash-sale, 154
Fluent Commerce, 107
Forevermark, 90
Fortnite, 81
Fulfilment, 67, 107–111, 154, 156
Full-stack ecosystem, xii, 141, 155, 158
Fused deposition modelling (FDM), xix, 105

G

Gamification, 5, 79, 81, 151, 152
GDPR, *see* General Data Privacy Regulation
Gemmyo, 104
Gemological Institute of America (GIA), xix, 115
General Data Privacy Regulation (GDPR), xix, 132, 149
Geo-localisation, 5

174 Index

GIA, *see* Gemological Institute of America
Gift cards, 45
Gilt, 39
Glocal, 57
Gold, 18–20, 25, 26, 55, 68, 89, 103–105, 111, 153
Google, 39, 54, 78, 82, 83, 126, 129, 130, 148
GPS, xx, 5, 85, 88
Gucci, 22, 37, 53, 74, 76, 117, 150, 152

H

Hapticmedia, 101
Harry Winston, 69, 89
Helzberg Diamonds, 87
HENRYs, 51, 53, 55
Hermés, 37, 53, 79, 100, 117, 122, 152, 153
Hero, 86
H&M, 53
Holograms, 74
Hublot, 27, 55, 74, 85, 115, 120, 151
Hybrid application, 126

I

iBeacons, 85, 88, 131
IBM, 107
Immersive, 7, 70, 72, 74, 85, 94
IMVU, 80
India, 23, 24, 29
Influencer, 44, 95
Initiatives, 143, 145
Innovation, xi, xii, 7, 10, 11, 35, 36, 45, 54, 55, 69, 71, 77, 85, 106, 113, 145, 151, 155, 156, 162
Inspify, 86
Inspiration, 4, 75, 83, 86, 104, 125
Instagram, 29, 43, 48, 69, 83, 84, 95
In-Store Data, 130

Internal data, 148
Intershop, 153
Inventory visibility, 109, 111, 112
iOS, 125
Iterative, 64, 127, 144, 151
IWC, 54, 85, 122

J

Jaeger LeCoultre, 55, 98
J*Art, 92
Japan, 23, 52
JD, 8, 45–47, 58, 86, 117
Jimmy Choo, 53

K

Kano model, 110
KBRW, 107
Kering, 9, 10, 22, 38, 41, 42, 60
Kibo, 107
Kimberley process, 55
KPI Tracking, 127–134
Kuaishou, 47, 78

L

LaoFengXiang, 24
LASE PeCo, 132
Laser sensors, 132
Last-mile, 116
League of Legends, 79
Lightbox, 55
LinkedIn, 161
Live chat, 156
Live-commerce, 106
Live streaming, 10, 46–48
Lode, 86, 94
Louis Vuitton, 23, 46, 53, 77–79, 100, 115, 120
Louvre, 78
Loyalty, 59, 63–65, 68, 76, 83, 89, 98, 115, 117–127, 131, 144, 161

Luisa Via Roma, 153
Luk Fook, 24
Luxury Pavilion, 47, 52, 58, 77, 154
LVMH, 10, 22, 38, 115, 146, 158

M

Mackevision, 71, 73
Magento, 153
Maison 203, 104
Manhattan, 107
Marc Jacobs, 77
Market consolidation, 8
Market growth, 1
Marketing, 19, 23, 28, 31, 35, 37, 44, 48, 54, 73, 76, 85, 87, 88, 94–97, 106, 109, 116, 119, 120, 122, 125, 129, 130, 132–134, 142, 146, 148–150
Master data management (MDM), xx, 133
MatchesFashion, 9, 38
Matomo, 130
MDM, see Master data management
Mechanical watches, 54
Memory, 63, 66
Metal, 18, 25, 73, 104, 105, 112, 113
Methodology, 133, 150
Microchip, 113, 114
Microsoft, 10, 96, 115, 133
Millennials, xii, 4, 46, 51–53, 55–60
Mini program, 46, 93
Mixed-reality, 7
Mobile app, 3, 7, 96, 124, 125, 131, 155
Mobile first, 4
Mobile phones, xii, 48, 77
Modular marketplace, xii, 141
Montblanc, 21, 53
Moqod, 92
Moschino, 80
Multi-brand, 41
Museums, 76, 78

Mystery shopping, 70
Mytheresa, 153

N

Narrative, 80, 86, 94
Native application, 125
Natural language processing (NLP), xx, 91
Near-field communication (NFC), xx, 26, 112, 113, 115
Near Infrared, xx, 6
Neiman Marcus, 38
Net-a-Porter, xx, 9, 23, 38, 58, 153
New retail, 1, 8, 12, 13, 45, 51, 58, 162
Newsletter, 4, 12, 84, 122, 148
NFC, see Near-field communication
NFT, see Non-fungible tokens
NLP, see Natural language processing
Non-fungible tokens (NFT), 74, 111

O

Objectives, 142, 144
Obsess, 94
Officine Panerai, 26, 104
Omega, 23, 24, 69, 122
Omni-channel, xi, 3–5, 12, 42, 47, 64, 66, 67, 69, 72, 85, 99, 107–112, 116, 124, 128, 130, 133, 134, 141, 146, 151–153, 155, 156, 158, 162
Omni-personal, xi, xii, 3, 5, 12, 13, 30, 42, 51, 60, 63–65, 89, 107, 111, 119, 129, 131, 134, 141–144, 146–152, 156, 161, 162
OMS, see Order management system
Online, xii, 1–4, 8, 10, 23, 35, 37, 38, 40–43, 47, 52, 56, 57, 64, 68, 69, 72, 77, 78, 83, 89, 91, 94, 96, 98–102, 104, 106, 110, 116, 118, 119, 122, 124, 127, 128, 130, 133, 134, 147, 153–156

Online data, 129
On-premises, 147
OpenSea, 80
Oracle, 133
OrderDynamics, 107
Order management system (OMS), xx, 107, 109, 133, 149
Oris, 71
Ownership, 2, 23, 40, 59, 74, 84, 89, 108, 112, 115, 125, 150

P

PaaS, *see* Platform as a service
Patek Philippe, 10, 23, 27, 30, 40, 78
Payments, 100
People, 4, 9, 22, 24, 27, 29, 82, 101, 145, 151–152
Periscope, 43
Personalisation, 3, 5, 19, 27, 52, 68, 77, 95, 97, 98, 101, 105, 110, 111, 121, 132, 144–146, 150, 155, 156, 158, 161, 162
Personal preferences, 60, 68, 70, 96, 146
Phygital, 5, 7, 35, 42, 43, 51, 70, 74, 76, 85, 93, 155
Piaget, 85
Pick and pack, 109
PIM, *see* Product information management
Pinterest, 83
Platform as a service (PaaS), xx, 147
Point Flottant, 73
Pokémon Go, 81
Pomellato, 21, 68, 69
Pop-in stores, 85
Pop-up stores, 76
Prada, 78, 87, 115
Predictive, 133
Privacy policy, 132
Processes, 145, 150–151
Prodject, 85

Product catalogue, 96, 101, 124
Product comparisons, 90
Product information management (PIM), xx, 67, 147, 148
Progressive (web) application, 126
Purple, 132

Q

Qeelin, 24
QQ, 44, 46
QR, xx, 85, 87, 110, 112, 113, 124, 129
Quytech, 92

R

Radio-frequency identification (RFID), xx, 26, 38, 85, 87, 112–114, 132, 155
Ralph Lauren, 87
The RealReal, 40
Real time, 7, 46, 48, 67, 85, 89, 125, 127, 131–134, 146, 147, 149, 156
Rebecca Minkoff, 87
Recommendation, 39, 68, 81, 101, 122
Relevance, 1, 5, 23, 24, 52, 67, 96, 106, 121, 127
Religion, 17, 19, 20, 31
Renèsim, 71
Rental, 6, 40, 51, 59, 60
Rent the Runway, 59
Resale, 6, 40, 51, 57, 59, 60
Responsibilities, 111, 150
Responsive AI, 89, 94
Return, xx, 107
Revolution, 20, 21
Reward, 22, 25, 29, 57, 81, 151
RFID, *see* Radio-frequency identification
Richard Mille, 69

Index

Richemont, 9, 11, 22, 38, 41, 42, 60, 115, 156
Roadmap, xii, 108, 162
Roger Dubuis, 27
Rolex, 23–25, 40, 41, 55, 102, 120, 153
ROPO, 89
Royals, 3, 20, 95, 100
Runways, 5, 10

S

SaaS, *see* Software as a service
Salesforce, 96, 133
Sales history, 12, 31, 67, 89, 97
Samesurf, 85
SAP Hybris, 153
Scalability, 8, 22, 41, 75, 91, 95, 116, 146
Search engine advertising (SEA), 82, 129
Search engine optimisation (SEO), 82, 83, 129
Second-hand platform, 9, 60
Secoo, 47
Segmentation, 43, 96, 148, 149
Sensalytics, 132
SEO, *see* Search engine optimisation
Ship from store, 109
Ship to store, 109
Shopping club, 39
SimplyBook, 91
Sims, 80
Singles' Day, 45
Skype, 85
SLA, *see* Stereolithography
Smart mirror, 74, 87
Smartphone, 4, 52, 79, 87, 126
Smartwatch, xii, 53–55, 113, 122
Snapchat, 43, 95
Social commerce, 44–48
Social listening, 122, 148

Social media, xii, 4, 12, 29, 42–48, 51, 55, 58, 76, 77, 79, 81–84, 87, 88, 94, 96, 97, 119, 122, 123, 129, 145, 148
Software as a service (SaaS), xx, 101, 147
Sourcing, 55, 107, 109, 112
Status, xi, xii, 18–20, 23, 26–28, 53, 57, 68, 125, 148
Stereolithography (SLA), xx, 105
STISS, *see* Swiss Technology Inside Smart Sapphire
Stocktaking, 114
Store pickup, 109
Store to store, 109
Storytelling, 26, 31, 75, 80
Stratasys, 104
Strategy, xii, 1, 8, 9, 19, 23–25, 27, 30, 33n16, 40, 52, 55, 58, 72, 75, 78, 104, 120, 122, 134, 141–144, 146, 150, 152, 156, 161
Subscription, 59, 60, 100, 122, 147
Sustainability, 2, 6, 11, 12, 25, 27, 40, 55, 59, 86, 111
Swarovski, 53, 61n3, 83
Swatch, 23, 113
Swiss Technology Inside Smart Sapphire (STISS), xx, 113

T

TAG Heuer, 24, 53
Talent, 146, 151
Taobao, 10, 47
Target segments, 142
Technology, xx, 10, 88, 94, 96, 113, 141, 143, 145–149
3D, 5, 26, 30, 73, 75, 77, 80, 98, 101, 103–105, 132, 147, 154
Threedium, 73
Tiffany, 21, 26, 37, 41, 55, 69, 77, 83, 95, 97, 111, 119

TikTok, 43, 44, 46, 48
Timevallée, 153
Timify, 91
Tmall, 47, 52, 58, 77, 86, 154
Touchpoints, xii, 3–5, 8, 10, 12, 31, 41, 57, 60, 63, 66, 67, 69, 73, 74, 107, 119, 122, 127, 149, 156
Traceability, 6, 111, 112, 116, 130
Tracr, 115, 116
Transformation, xi, xii, xvii, 1, 2, 24, 37, 56, 58, 64, 70, 73, 141, 142, 145, 146, 150, 151, 153, 156, 162
Transparency, 6, 36, 40, 55, 111, 112, 114–116, 129, 156
Tryon, 5, 40, 68, 71, 74, 75, 80, 92, 107, 124
24S, 153
Twitter, 43, 46

U

Ultraleap, 86
Ulysse Nardin, 120
United States, 2, 35, 40, 45
Usability, 127
User-generated content, 44, 95

V

Vacheron Constantin, 57, 115, 125
Value chain, 5, 6, 10, 19, 31, 73, 111, 114–116, 143, 145, 154, 158
Van Cleef & Arpels, 119, 158
Van Herpen, Iris, 104
Vente-Privée, 23, 39, 154
Verenia, 102
Versace, 53
Vertical integration, xii
Vestiaire Collective, 9, 40, 60
Video cameras, 132
Virtual agents, 91

Virtual model, 80
Virtual Reality (VR), xx, 70–76, 92, 97, 100

W

Walkbase, 132
Watchdreamer, 59
Watchfinder, 40, 60
Web application, 126
Webmosphere, 89, 94
WeChat, 4, 7, 8, 10, 43, 44, 46, 57, 83, 87, 93, 96, 97, 100, 155
Weibo, 43, 44, 46
Wempe, 153
White-glove, 47, 58, 117
Wi-Fi trackers, 132
Wish list, 12, 89, 90, 94, 96, 98, 102, 105, 124, 125, 146, 148
WIseKey, 115

X

Xiaodian, 46
Xiaohongshu, 10, 46

Y

Yizhibo, 10, 46
YNAP, *see* Yoox Net-a-Porter
Yoox, xx, 9, 38, 41
Yoox Net-a-Porter (YNAP), xx, 9, 38, 39, 41, 42, 47, 58, 117, 118, 153–156
Youku, 44
Younger generations, 4, 40, 71, 72, 79, 91
YouTube, 43, 48, 54, 78, 80, 121

Z

Zenith, 91
Zhaoyi Jade, 24
Zoom, 85